Raspberry Pi Retail Applications

Transform Your Business with a Low-Cost Single-Board Computer

Elaine Wu
Dmitry Maslov

Apress®

Raspberry Pi Retail Applications: Transform Your Business with a Low-Cost Single-Board Computer

Elaine Wu
Shenzhen, China

Dmitry Maslov
Shenzhen, China

ISBN-13 (pbk): 978-1-4842-7950-2
https://doi.org/10.1007/978-1-4842-7951-9

ISBN-13 (electronic): 978-1-4842-7951-9

Managing Director, Apress Media LLC: Welmoed Spahr
Acquisitions Editor: Aaron Black
Development Editor: James Markham
Coordinating Editor: Jessica Vakili
Copy Editor: Kezia Endsley

Distributed to the book trade worldwide by Springer Science+Business Media New York, 233 Spring Street, 6th Floor, New York, NY 10013. Phone 1-800-SPRINGER, fax (201) 348-4505, e-mail orders-ny@springer-sbm.com, or visit www.springeronline.com. Apress Media, LLC is a California LLC and the sole member (owner) is Springer Science + Business Media Finance Inc (SSBM Finance Inc). SSBM Finance Inc is a **Delaware** corporation.

For information on translations, please e-mail booktranslations@springernature.com; for reprint, paperback, or audio rights, please e-mail bookpermissions@springernature.com.

Apress titles may be purchased in bulk for academic, corporate, or promotional use. eBook versions and licenses are also available for most titles. For more information, reference our Print and eBook Bulk Sales web page at http://www.apress.com/bulk-sales.

Any source code or other supplementary material referenced by the author in this book is available to readers on the Github repository: https://github.com/Apress/Raspberry-Pi-Retail-Applications. For more detailed information, please visit http://www.apress.com/source-code.

Printed on acid-free paper

Table of Contents

About the Authors

Elaine Wu specializes in business partnerships and marketing in various tech industries, from software to embedded hardware. She is currently the marketing and partnership manager at Seeed (an open-source AIoT hardware platform) where she focuses on the global IoT solution ecosystem, making technology accessible for all. At Seeed, by aligning with partners and best hardware, she believes and strives on the path of the most reliable hardware platform, empowering everyone to achieve their digital transformation goals. She was also leading community partnerships, content marketing, new products' go-to-market strategies at Seeed before 2021. Elaine is an active article contributor at Seeed blog on a variety of industries topics, including but not limited to SBCs, microcontrollers, ML/AI, robotics, and SLAM.

Dmitry Maslov works professionally in applied machine learning and robotics. He has spearheaded a variety of machine learning projects, both for previous employers and as a freelancer. Proficient in Python and C/C++, Dmitry has an excellent knowledge of ROS and ROS-i. He speaks four languages, with professional fluency in three. Dmitry is the owner of Hardware.ai, a YouTube channel where he publishes videos on creating intelligent systems with machine learning and ROS on single-board computers.

About the Technical Reviewer

Massimo Nardone has more than 22 years of experience in security, web/mobile development, and cloud and IT architecture. His true IT passions are security and the Android platform.

He has been programming and teaching others how to program with Android, Perl, PHP, Java, VB, Python, C/C++, and MySQL for more than 20 years.

He holds an MS in Computing Science from the University of Salerno, Italy.

He has worked as a project manager, software engineer, research engineer, chief security architect, information security manager, PCI/SCADA auditor, and senior lead IT security/cloud/SCADA architect for many years.

.

CHAPTER 1

Understanding the Applications of Automation in Retail

What are some of the most pressing issues that owners of small- and medium-sized businesses currently face?

These concerns include the growing costs of supply chains, increasing costs of labor and capital, and increased spending on equipment upgrades and business strategy re-evaluations necessitated by competitors and changes in the business environment. It is very important for small business owners to have solid and practical solutions for saving money on manufacturing processes and labor. They need to increase efficiency and widen the margin in both directions—by eliminating unnecessary expenses and by increasing revenues.

With the development of Industry 4.0, the automation of business retail applications has been gaining interest and popularity. Automation in retail applications reshapes the business models, from the backend supply chain to the frontend of business management, which not only helps business owners save on labor costs, but also helps with efficiency. With automation, customers can have a better experience in an easier way.

© Elaine Wu, Dmitry Maslov 2022
E. Wu and D. Maslov, *Raspberry Pi Retail Applications*,
https://doi.org/10.1007/978-1-4842-7951-9_1

What Is Industry 4.0?

Industry 4.0, the fourth industrial revolution, refers to the ongoing digital transformation of industries, such as combining human machine interface (HMI) and cloud data to build digital solutions to make the industrial model more efficient (see Figure 1-1). Compared to the preceding industrial revolutions, Industry 4.0 focuses on the digital, information-driven interconnectivity among people, devices, and systems, which enables enhanced decision making in industrial processes. At the same time, due to this digital transformation, customer expectations are rising. Retailers are striving to adapt and survive in a competitive environment. With Industry 4.0, a lot of new skills must be added to the development and manufacturing process, such as machine learning capabilities, edge computing, and remotely visualized dashboards using cloud businesses. Retail owners at the same time must use new technology to make solid decisions about hardware and software.

The Four Industrial Revolutions

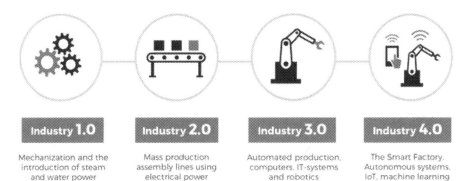

Figure 1-1. *The four industrial revolutions. Source: Spectral Engines*

McKinsey & Company, "COVID-19: An Inflection Point for Industry 4.0" is a survey of more than 400 global manufacturing companies. A full 94% of the respondents said that Industry 4.0 helped them to maintain operations during COVID-19 (starting from the end of 2019), and 56% of the respondents said that digitization was crucial to responding to the pandemic. See Figure 1-2.

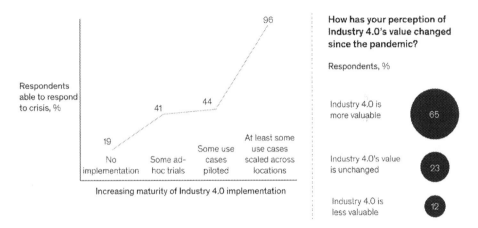

Figure 1-2. *Companies that implemented Industry 4.0 report a stronger ability to respond to pandemic crises. Source: McKinsey & Company, "COVID-19: An inflection Point for Industry 4.0"*

According to Deloitte's report (see Figure 1-3), Industry 4.0 originated in Europe and developed rapidly in Germany's manufacturing sectors. Across the United States, Industry 4.0 may be translated into the concept of "industrial Internet" and "Internet of Things." Since the 1970s, industrial progress has increasingly embraced automation.

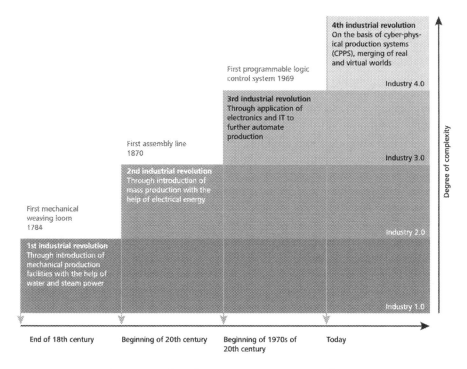

Figure 1-3. *Definition of Industry 4.0. Source: Deloitte*

We believe that single-board computers such as the Raspberry Pi can motivate and inspire retailers to faster digital transformation, because the Raspberry Pi lowers the barriers from development to deployment. In the longer term, when large enterprises need transformation and small retail businesses need expansion, companies also need to invest in the appropriate infrastructure, such as research and development (R&D) and procurement units, in order to successfully realize the digital transformation of Industry 4.0. Procurement, production, warehousing, and logistics are at the core of the digital transformation of Industry 4.0, as everything becomes convenient. Sales and service departments stand to gain the most from the result of Industry 4.0. In these market segments, more customized solutions can bring the manufacturing and retail business industries into a new era of customization.

What Is the Internet of Things (IoT)?

The Internet of Things (IoT) is the connection between the digital world and the physical world. IoT is a network of physical objects ("things") embedded with sensors, software, and other technologies, which helps exchange data with devices through different communication networks. These devices can come from households (lamps, speakers, and kitchen tools) or from industrial machines (manufacturing equipment and fleets). IoT syncs the digital world and real-world data. This digitization of the physical world is creating new value for customers.

The potential economic value that IoT may realize is huge and growing. It is estimated that by 2030 (McKinsey & Company, "Potential Economic Value of the IoT"), including the value that consumers obtain through IoT products and services, IoT is expected to create a value of 5.5-12.6 trillion U.S. dollars worldwide.

Which Technologies Make the Internet of Things More Accessible in the Retail Industry?

- *Low-cost, low-power sensors:* Devices can collect environmental changes, motion, and other data in the retail environment to help retailers make better decisions faster.

- *Real-world data collection:* Machines supporting IoT can initiate commands, such as payment and identification commands.

- *Ubiquitous connectivity:* A large number of connection protocols—such as BLE, WiFi, Zigbee, LoRa, LTE, and 5G—make it more efficient and cost-effective to connect sensors to devices, the cloud, and to "things" around us.

- *Cloud computing platform:* The cloud platform ensures the stable operation of the infrastructure. The cloud platform provides fully managed services, ingesting and processing the data from millions of distributed devices around the world.

- *Machine learning integration:* Embedded machine learning helps to operate and analyze massive amounts of data much faster. Business owners can gather insights easier with reliable data models.

- *Speech recognition:* Natural language processing (NLP) integrated into IoT devices can be deployed directly in offices and homes as home automation.

According to Microsoft's industry blog, *"5 IoT Retail Trends for 2021,"* Carl Norberg, Founder of Turnpike, stated "We realized that by connecting store IoT sensors, POS systems, and AI cameras, store staff can be empowered to interact at the right place at the right time."

McKinsey & Company's research ("IoT Value Set to Accelerate Through 2030") in November of 2021 demonstrated that the IoT offers significant economic value potential through 2030. In the retail environment, the research predicted that self-checkouts (billing, payments, and material handling) and real-time personalized promotions will be the top uses for retail industry adoption of IoT. See Figure 1-4.

Figure 1-4. *Estimated 2030 economic value of IoT adoption, by setting, billion dollars, retail environment segment. Source: McKinsey & Company, "IoT Value Set to Accelerate Through 2030"*

Although the potential economic value of IoT is considerable, the actual deployment and final transformation are equally challenging, especially in a B2B (business-to-business) environment. Many companies have been struggling to transition from pilot projects to successful large-scale deployments in order to obtain breakthrough value.

The IoT technology is connecting the digital world to the physical world. Manufacturers and companies may take advantage of IoT to improve operations, manage tangible assets, and enhance customer experience. IoT is becoming the core of digital transformation. There has also been an increasing need for industrial-grade IoT products, as many industries are going through the digital transformation.

Based on the research of well-known consulting companies, authors' experience in the IoT field, and familiarity with latest hardware resources, we hope to give employers in the retail industry who are still in the exploring stage confidence to move to the proof of concept (PoC) stage now, as well as help retail employers accelerate their digital transformation.

Amazon Go Grocery Store: Ambitiously Implementing Automation

If you visit an Amazon Go grocery store, you will find that there are no human interactions. You just walk in, scan the QR codes with the Amazon mobile app, put anything you want to purchase into your basket, and finally walk out when you are finished shopping. The store only staffs a few employees to inventory shelves and answer shoppers' questions, but there is almost no human interaction (see Figures 1-5 and 1-6).

> *Amazon reportedly had been forecasting annual revenue from all Amazon Go stores would skyrocket from $28 million in 2018 to upwards of $639 million in 2020, according to The Information. But Amazon hasn't opened as many Go stores as it had initially anticipated, the report said. And operating losses from Go are still ballooning, it said.*
>
> —CNBC: "Amazon is opening its first full-size, cashierless grocery store. Here's a first look inside"

Figure 1-5. *The "just walk in, just walk out" technology builds on what Amazon has learned with its smaller Go stores. Source: Lauren Thomas, CNBC*

Figure 1-6. *Amazon Dash Cart. Source: Amazon*

The Amazon Dash Cart (see Figure 1-6) helps with the "walk-in and walk-out" process launched by Amazon's Go store. There are hundreds of cameras on the ceiling to track your every move. In your basket, there is a built-in scale, cameras, and sensors to calculate what you put in the basket. A Dash Cart can hold two bags. When you finish your purchase, Dash Cart links to your Amazon account to deduct the corresponding payment. There is a screen on the top to display the shopping list and you can even scan coupons. Can you implement the Dash Cart idea by using Raspberry Pi and sensors and deploy it with machine learning? Later chapters will return to this question.

Why Choose a $35 Single-Board Computer to Automate a Retail Business?

It is surprising that, with a $35 credit card-sized, single-board computer, retailers can increase productivity and lower operational costs. This is possible simply by automating crucial business processes.

Raspberry Pi, the most popular and affordable credit card-sized, single-board computer, is available in multiple form factors. You can get it as a development board, as a system on module (SoM), and as an all-in-one personal computer kit with a keyboard. Figures 1-7 through 1-9 show various aspects of the Raspberry Pi board.

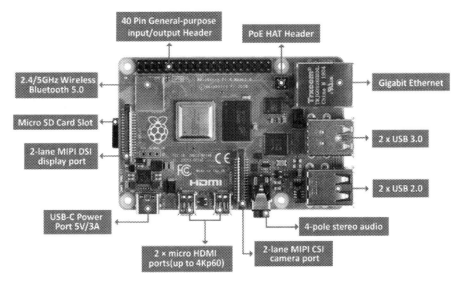

Figure 1-7. *Raspberry Pi 4 hardware overview. Source: Seeed*

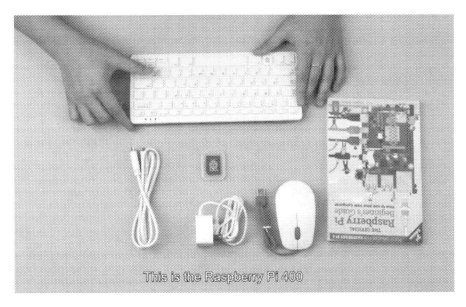

Figure 1-8. *Raspberry Pi 400 | All-In-One RPI with keyboard and mouse, reviewed by Seeed. Source: Seeed*

Figure 1-9. *The new Raspberry Pi Compute Module 4 by Raspberry Pi. Source: Raspberry Pi*

Whether you are still developing ideas to transform your business or you have an idea but lack the skill to implement it, this book is an invaluable resource for you to navigate the ever-changing landscape of retail automation.

Identify the Targets for Business Automation

What can automation do at the current level of technical progress? This list explains many of the current targets of automation:

- *Predictive analysis:* This is a common approach to managing and automating business processes. It can be also used to automate routine tasks in retail businesses by replacing human decisions with machine decisions. One of the most powerful use cases is the automation of routine decisions based on big data analysis.

Retailers can use machine vision algorithms to detect the movement of customers in the store. These algorithms detect when a customer enters the store, when a customer leaves the store, when a customer is walking in the store, when a customer is walking toward or away from a product, when a customer stops near a product, and so on.

- *Tracking and analyzing data from sensors:* By grabbing environmental data from the sensors, retailers can implement and send data to the cloud to run analytics. For example, a retail store can grab data from a sensor to track customer behaviors. If a sensor is tracking the customers' walking patterns, the system can suggest products that the customers might be interested in. The system can also track customers from their walking patterns and send notifications based on the customer's behavior. For example, if a customer looks at a product for a long time, the system will send information about that product to the customer's mobile device. This can be a great way to increase the conversion with potential consumers.

Student can learn about data-driven farming using AI, Machine learning and IoT with with FarmBeats Raspberry Pi Kit. Source: Seeed. Train apps to distinguish various plants. Source: Lobe.

- *Automated marketing:* You can automate your marketing communications with customers. You can create customer segments based on their interests, send them targeted messages, and run retargeting campaigns.

- *Automated customer service:* You can use NLP and speech-to-text to automate the customer service experience.

- *IT service management:* This can assist in the design, planning, delivery, operation, and control of all activities through the whole service process offered to customers. For example, with the help of Jira Service Management (see Figure 1-12), you can easily receive, track, manage, respond, and resolve customer requests. Customers can send requests via email and embedded plug-ins. Jira Service Management will systematically organize these requests in one place, and then prioritize requests to decide which to execute.

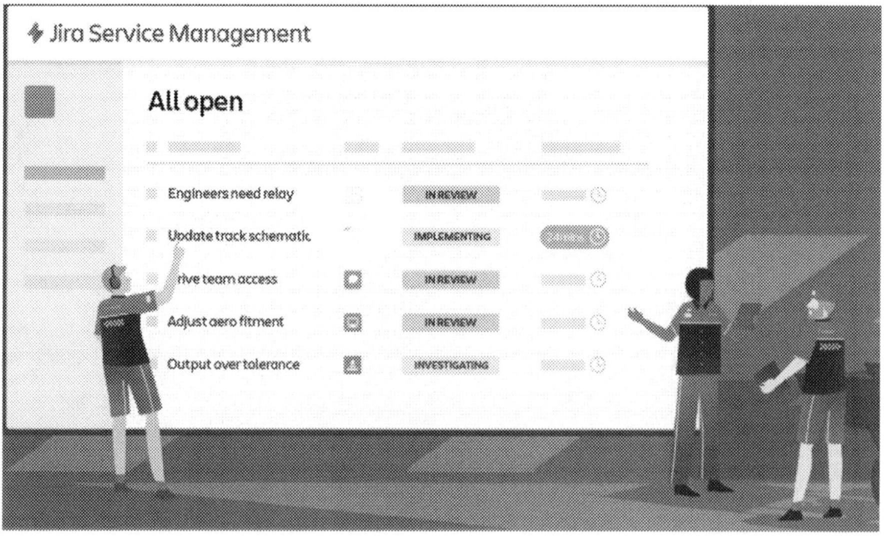

Figure 1-10. *Jira Service Management*

To Automate or Not to Automate?

Before implementing automation into your retail business, it is very important to understand the limitations of the current technologies. While some automation targets might seem lucrative and in theory could provide significant gains due to efficiency, you may discover that the modern technological stack is not sufficient to achieve your desired goals.

For example, say your customers want to talk to customer service during their online shopping process, but the chatbots automatically respond to these conversations without correctly responding to the complicated questions. In this case, your users may feel it's a waste of time when interacting with chatbots. Likewise, when we call the bank, there is often too much waiting time for automatic problem identification. When we book a hotel or travel itinerary online, we don't like to wait for a conversation with a bot agent. It often takes a lot of the customer's time to drill through the menus and get the appropriate help. Customers may hang up or disconnect with indignation. The worst result is when customers blacklist a company or service due to the poor level of service they received.

Speech recognition and computer vision applications are not yet 100% accurate when it comes to automation. In later chapters, we use real examples to show how computer vision can be effectively applied in the retail business using Raspberry Pi, so that you can take reference to your business.

> *"Conversational AI is in many ways the ultimate AI. Deep learning breakthroughs in speech recognition, language understanding, and speech synthesis have enabled engaging cloud services. NVIDIA Jarvis brings this state-of-the-art conversational AI out of the cloud for customers to host AI services anywhere."*

—Jensen Huang, Founder and CEO of NVIDIA, GTC2021 keynote

When looking for automation solutions, some key points to consider are:

- What are the reasons to choose automation?

- How much time will it take to integrate automation?

- How much time will it take to adapt the automation solution to the existing processes?

- How many business units will it impact?

- How many users will it impact?

- Will automation simplify the user experience, or will it complicate it?

- Will automation be able to reduce the support costs?

Apart from picking the right target for automation, when you're trying to integrate several different technologies into the workflow, it is important also to choose the right tools and technologies and not over-engineer the project. You can always add new tools and technologies later, but you will surely regret not having the most appropriate tools and technologies right from the start.

Choosing Tools

When it comes to choosing the right tools for your project, you should never sacrifice flexibility for ease of use. The best tools are not necessarily easy to use, but they are flexible and allow you to extend their functionality without losing time. One of the most common examples of this behavior is using Python for automation, while C is the most popular programming language required for automation development. Python is very easy to learn, but it is not as fast as C, which is more complex. However, Python allows developers to write less code, which makes it more flexible. Also, when your project uses open-source technologies, you can easily find developers with the necessary skills to extend your solution's functionality.

Choosing Technologies

Choosing the right technologies for your project is not an easy task. You must remember that all technologies are not created equal. If you're struggling to find the right technology, the best way to approach the problem is to think about your current and future needs. For this, you need to know your own business, the nature of the work you're doing, and what you need to achieve with automation. Then, you can consider which technologies can help you achieve your goals.

The retail industry is changing rapidly. New generations of customers are expecting more personalization and convenience. This is why more and more retailers are looking for ways to optimize their services. Automation can help turn your retail business into a successful and profitable company. It can provide you with the tools and technologies to provide your customers with personalized and seamless experiences, which is a great investment. With the right approach and having a clear goal in your mind, you can achieve great results with automation.

We hope that you will gain valuable knowledge about the potential applications shared in the following chapters. You should conduct a thorough analysis to understand the best way to quickly apply automation to your existing systems and processes. You can apply the helpful suggestions on extending the lessons and projects in this book to other types of retail and application scenarios.

CHAPTER 2

People Counting

Problem Overview

The number of customers that visit a store greatly affects its retail profits, but the traditional ways of assessing customer flow have been prone to error. Computer vision techniques can automate the process of people counting and reporting. The solutions available on the market currently cost at least a few hundred dollars and most often are closed-source, which raises privacy concerns. This chapter analyzes and implements a deep learning-based people counting solution using the Raspberry Pi 4 and a ceiling-mounted, top-view camera. This solution is based on open source technology, it's easy to implement and maintain, and it has the additional benefit of costing a little over 50 dollars.

The Business Impact

Having data about customer flow during different time periods is crucial to optimizing resource allocation. Management can make decisions about staffing at certain times and in certain parts of the store based on customer flow data, which can help prevent overstaffing/understaffing and can raise customer satisfaction rates. Of course, the impact of customer flow data is not limited to people-management decisions; it can also be used to improve store logistics (when multiple counting devices are installed near different aisles/hallways) and inventory stocking.

Related Knowledge

The most traditional approach to people counting of course is to have a dedicated person count the number of people entering and leaving the facility. No technical skills are required, but the disadvantages are very much obvious—the need and cost to allocate a person's time and low accuracy over long periods of time, since people tend to get tired and take breaks and so on.

You can also use traditional sensors for people counting, such as ultrasonic/time-of-flight or infrared sensors installed in door frames. These solutions are more accurate and cost-effective, but also more limited. Since all of these sensors essentially check the distance to an obstacle, they can misread objects near them as a person coming or going. In addition, incoming and outgoing people streams need to be separated between different doors in order for the count to be accurate. In addition, since the height of detection is fixed, it might not work equally for people of different heights or for children.

Computer Vision and Its Applications

A more robust approach utilizes cameras and computer vision. Computer vision, often abbreviated as CV, is defined as a field of study that seeks to develop techniques to help computers "see" and understand the content of digital images, such as photographs and videos. It is a multidisciplinary field that can broadly be called a subfield of artificial intelligence and machine learning, which may involve the use of specialized methods and general learning algorithms. See Figure 2-1.

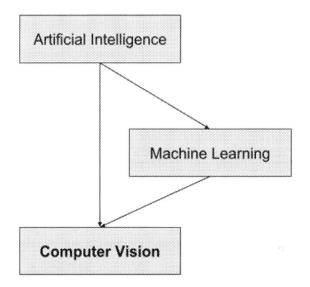

Figure 2-1. *The relationship between AI, machine learning, and computer vision*

One particular problem in computer vision may be easily addressed with a hand-crafted statistical method, whereas another may require a large and complex ensemble of generalized machine learning algorithms.

A 2010 textbook on computer vision entitled *Computer Vision: Algorithms and Applications* by Richard Szeliski provides a list of some high-level problems that have seen success using computer vision:

- Optical character recognition (OCR)

- Machine inspection

- Retail (e.g., automated checkouts)

- 3D model building (photogrammetry)

- Medical imaging

- Automotive safety

- Match move (e.g., merging CGI with live actors
  in movies)

- Motion capture (mocap)

- Surveillance

- Fingerprint recognition and biometrics

Many popular computer vision applications involve trying to recognize
things in photographs or videos, for example:

- **Image classification**: What broad category of object is
  in this photograph?

- **Object detection**: Where are the objects in the
  photograph?

- **Semantic segmentation**: What pixels belong to the
  object in the image?

Think for a moment—which of these is most applicable to the task of
people counting?

The right answer is *object detection.* Output of an image classification
algorithm is just an object category, in this case it would be "a person." It
cannot tell us where this person is or how many people there are. Semantic
segmentation would provide a pixel-by-pixel classification for the original
image. Although it might be suitable for people-counting tasks, it would
add unnecessary complexity.

Traditional computer vision algorithms can be used for people
detection, such as HOG descriptors or even simple frame differencing
to detect motion. When referring to "traditional" computer vision, we
mean hand-crafted algorithms consisting of complicated code written by
specialists in the field that take into account the inherent complexity of
visual perception. The opposite of traditional computer vision algorithms
involves using machine learning and deep learning in particular. See
Figure 2-2.

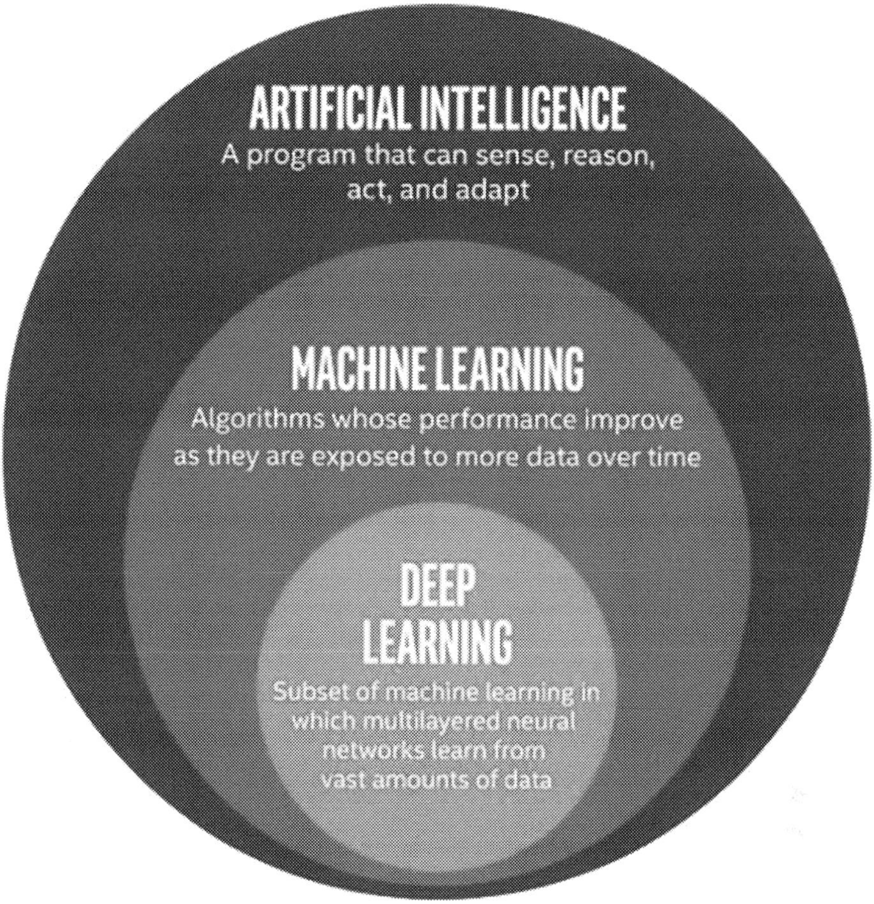

ARTIFICIAL INTELLIGENCE
A program that can sense, reason, act, and adapt

MACHINE LEARNING
Algorithms whose performance improve as they are exposed to more data over time

DEEP LEARNING
Subset of machine learning in which multilayered neural networks learn from vast amounts of data

Figure 2-2. *Deep learning description, as related to machine learning and artificial intelligence*

Machine learning studies and creates algorithms that can learn rules from data, be it tabular data, sound, or images. Deep learning is a narrower subset of machine learning, utilizing deep neural networks that can statistically learn general rules from vast amounts of data. Deep learning rose to popularity after a deep neural network created by Geoffrey Hinton achieved an extraordinarily high score in the ImageNet image classification competition in 2012. Deep learning moved to the spotlight of computer science and machine learning and is being used widely for a variety of tasks.

Approaches to Object Detection

There are numerous neural network architectures for object detection. One of the earlier approaches is exemplified in the Region Based Convolutional Neural Networks (R-CNN) architecture. Given an input image, R-CNN begins by applying a mechanism called *selective search* to extract regions of interest (ROI). Each ROI is a rectangle that represents the boundary of an object in an image. See Figure 2-3.

R-CNN: *Regions with CNN features*

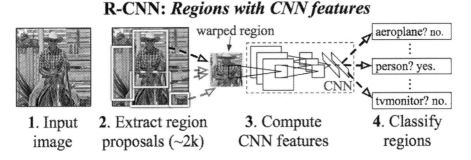

| 1. Input image | 2. Extract region proposals (~2k) | 3. Compute CNN features | 4. Classify regions |

Figure 2-3. *Working principle of an R-CNN diagram, Source: R-CNN, Fast R-CNN, Faster R-CNN, YOLO — Object Detection Algorithms*

Depending on the scenario, there may be as many as 2,000 ROIs. Each ROI is fed through a neural network to produce output features. For each ROI's output features, a collection of support-vector machine classifiers is used to determine what type of object (if any) is contained in the ROI.

Although R-CNN could achieve good accuracy on a variety of object detection benchmarks, the main disadvantage of this architecture was that multiple passes over the regions of interest were required. That meant that it was computationally expensive, which limited its usefulness in embedded systems.

The next step in the evolution of object detection networks were *single shot detectors* or SSDs, such as the very well-known YOLO (You Only Look Once) architecture. As expressed in the name, single shot detectors detect objects in the image in a single pass. Let's see how this is done using YOLOv2, which we are going to use later for person detection.

YOLOv2 divides images into a grid and predicts the presence (or absence) of an object in each grid cell. See Figure 2-4.

Figure 2-4. *An example of detection boxes in an image divided into a 3x3 grid*

To streamline and speed up the training process, so-called anchors or priors are provided to the network. Anchors are initial sizes (width, height) of bounding boxes, which are resized to the detected object size.

Here's a top-level view on what's going on when a YOLO architecture neural network performs object detection on the image. According to the features detected by the feature extractor network, for each grid cell, a set of predictions is made, which includes the anchor's offset, anchor probability, and anchor class. The predictions with low probabilities are discarded and you get a set of final predictions.

Once a person or multiple people are detected, it tracks each instance of the person and assigns a unique ID to them. It also tracks the direction of each ID. If an ID crosses the divisor line, YOLO counts the ID as entering or leaving the area.

Before we start with a practical implementation, it is important to mention the limitations of this technique. As you may know, no single method can handle all situations. The computer vision approach performs very well in brightly lit, uncluttered environments, when the camera is installed above the detection area at 70-90 degree angle. It will not perform that well if the line of sight is obstructed or in situations when large numbers of people (5~10) simultaneously leave or enter the area. In the second case, it will still count people, but the counting accuracy might decrease.

Implementing Object Detection

In this section you learn how to:

1) Install a 64-bit Raspberry Pi OS image on Raspberry Pi 4.

2) Install the necessary packages.

3) Execute people counting code with a pretrained MobileNet SSD model.

4) Train and optimize your own neural network model, which is specifically for people detection from a top-view camera.

Install a 64-bit Raspberry Pi OS on Raspberry Pi 4

For this particular project, you're going to use Raspberry Pi OS 64-bit instead of the 32-bit Raspberry Pi OS, since 64-bit support is particularly important for efficient, optimized execution of a neural network inference with TensorFlow Lite.

Raspberry Pi recommends that you use the Raspberry Pi Imager to install an operating system on your SD card. You need another computer with an SD card reader to install the image.

Using the Raspberry Pi Imager

Raspberry Pi has developed a graphical SD card writing tool that works on macOS, Ubuntu 18.04, and Windows called Raspberry Pi Imager. This is the easiest option for most users, since it will download the image automatically and install it to the SD card.

Download the latest version of Raspberry Pi Imager from `www.raspberrypi.com/software/` and install it on your main computer. The exact installation instructions depend on your OS. Additionally, since the 64-bit image was still in the development stage at the moment of writing this book, you'll need to download it manually from `https://downloads.raspberrypi.org/raspios_lite_arm64/images/`. The exact image used for the projects in this book was `2021-05-07-raspios-buster-arm64-lite.zip`.

Insert the SD card into your PC and run the Raspberry Pi Imager. Click Choose OS and scroll down to Use Custom, as shown in Figure 2-5.

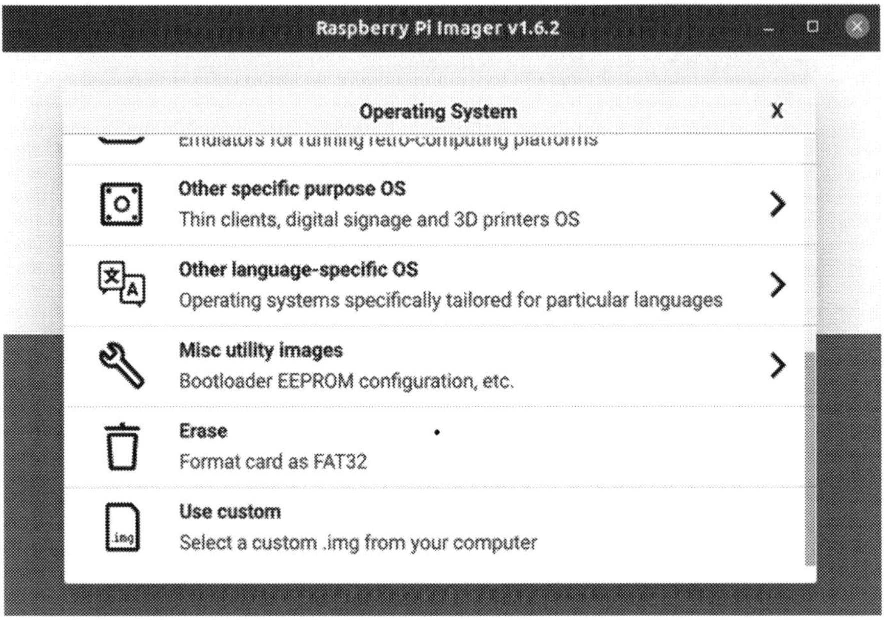

Figure 2-5. *Choosing a custom image in Raspberry Pi Imager*

Choose the `raspios-buster-arm64-lite.zip` archive you downloaded. Since you're going to use the Raspberry Pi *headless*, meaning without a keyboard and screen connected, it is necessary to enable SSH and specify the WiFi network name and password (if you want to connect the Raspberry Pi to the Internet with WiFi). You can do all of that by entering the Advanced options (choose Ctrl+Shift+X). See Figure 2-6.

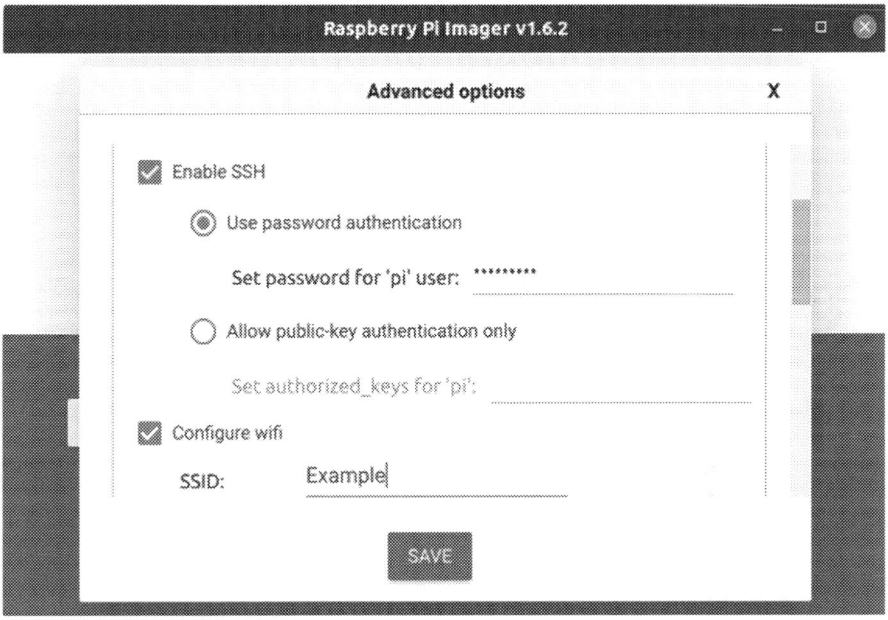

Figure 2-6. *Advanced configuration in Raspberry Pi Imager*

Save the changes and click the Write button in the Raspberry Pi Imager tool. After a few minutes, the flash process should be complete and you can eject the SD card and insert it into your Raspberry Pi 4.

Install the Necessary Packages

Since you are running the Raspberry Pi 4 headless, you need a convenient way to edit code and move files to and from Raspberry Pi 4. You could use your OS built-in SSH client and access the development boards simply by typing:

```
ssh pi@[your-pi-ip-address]
```

And entering the password. You can find your Raspberry Pi 4 IP address after it is powered on and connected to your router in your router configuration page (normally in the DHCP Client section, but this differs with different router models). See Figure 2-7.

29

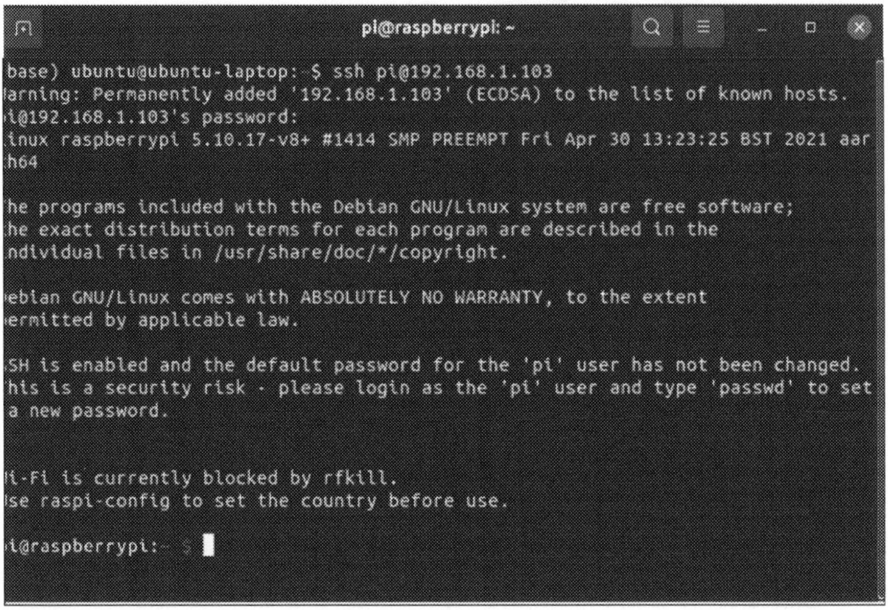

Figure 2-7. Accessing Raspberry PI 4 by using the default SSH client in Ubuntu 20.04

Instead, we recommend using Visual Studio Code, together with the official extension, Remote - SSH. This will allow you to edit code in a more powerful and comfortable IDE and transfer files between the Pi and the computer using a graphical user interface.

To install Visual Studio Code, go to `https://code.visualstudio.com/` and follow the installation instructions for your platform. After launching Visual Studio Code, click Extensions and search for Remote - SSH. After a short installation and Visual Studio Code restart, you will see a green button in the bottom-left corner, which allows you to connect to a remote device. See Figure 2-8.

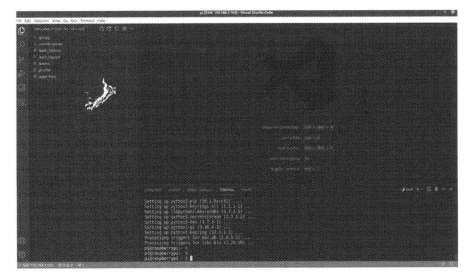

Figure 2-8. *Click the green button to start the SSH connection configuration*

Click that button, choose Connect Current Window to Host, then choose Add New SSH Host. After that, type pi@[your-pi-ip-address]. Click the green button again, then choose Connect Current Window to Host, and then choose pi@[your-pi-ip-address]. That will start the connection process. Click Open Folder and then OK for the default choice (normally /home/pi/). See Figure 2-9.

Figure 2-9. *Visual Studio Code interface after successful SSH connection*

Note   If your Raspberry Pi 4 IP address changes, you need to add the new SSH host again.

Raspberry Pi OS Image comes preinstalled with Python, along with other important software to get the project up and running. However, you need to manually install pip (Python Package Manager) for Python 3. You can do that by executing the following commands:

```
sudo apt-get update
sudo apt-get install python3-pip git
```

To install the necessary packages, `git` `clone` the repository for this book, then run these commands:

```
cd Chapter_2
pip3 install --upgrade pip
pip3 install --extra-index-url https://google-coral.github.io/
py-repo/ tflite_runtime
pip3 install - r requirements.txt
```

The second command will download and install all the necessary Python packages to your Raspberry Pi.

Execute People Counting Code with a Pretrained MobileNet SSD Model

First, you're going to use a readily-available MobileNet SSD model trained on a Pascal VOC dataset to detect objects of 20 different classes, including people. You can find the code for this exercise in the `Chapter_2/Exercise_1` folder. Let's go through the most important pieces of code.

`detector_video.py` is the main script, inside of which you import the TensorFlow Lite interpreter, the Flask web server, and other helper

packages and functions. You'll create a web app, which will render an
`index.html` template with an image placeholder. This image placeholder
will access the `/video_stream` route of the app, which yields processed
video streams from the camera.

After acquiring a frame with OpenCV, you pass it to the method of the
detector instance of the `Detector` class you initialized earlier. The image
is preprocessed and makes a forward pass through the neural network
model. You parse the results in the `run` method of the `Detector` class.
Then, in the `draw_overlay()` method, for each detected bounding box,
you check if the box centroids are sufficiently close to centroids of other
IDs, which are already registered and kept track of using the `self.people_
list` list.

If these centroids are sufficiently close (Euclidean distance between
the two pairs of coordinates is used as a metric), you assign an existing
ID to them; if they are not, you assign a new ID to that bounding box.
Additionally, if an ID coordinate is not updated during a set amount of
frames, you delete it from the `self.people_list` list. Each ID also has a
direction property associated with it, which is calculated as the moving
average of the last 12 y-coordinates of the ID. So, if the ID has been moving
up the image, it will have a positive direction and if it has been moving
down the image, the ID will have a negative direction. The program uses
that property to count people as leaving or entering, when they cross
a central line. If the person's ID is moving up the image (in a positive
direction) and is above the central line, it counts them as entering. If the
person's ID is moving down the image (in a negative direction) and is
below the central line, it counts them as leaving. The leaving-entering
direction can be swapped if desired.

Finally, you draw centroids, boxes for each ID, and display the total
number of people who entered and left using OpenCV drawing functions
on the screen.

To check the model and the script on the example video, run the following command from the Exercise_1 folder:

```
python3 detector_video.py --model models/MobileNet-
YOLOv2-224_224.tflite --labels models/MobileNet-YOLOv2-224_224.
txt --source file --file ../video_samples/example_01.mp4
```

Then open the http://[your-pi-ip-address]:5000/ web page. Your Raspberry Pi needs to be on the same network as your computer. You will see the output of the video stream displayed in the web browser, as shown in Figure 2-10.

Figure 2-10. *Inference on a prerecorded video file*

To use the stream from the web camera, enter the following command on your Raspberry Pi:

```
python3 detector_video.py --model models/MobileNet-YOLOv2-224
_224.tflite --labels models/MobileNet-YOLOv2-224_224.txt --source cv
```

Finally, to use a PiCamera module, use this command:

```
python3 detector_video.py --model models/MobileNet-YOLOv2-224_224
.tflite --labels models/MobileNet-YOLOv2-224_224.txt --source
picamera
```

What you will see is that the performance of the detection model is better when used on frontal images of people. This is because it is a generic detection model trained on a Pascal VOC dataset to detect 20 classes of different objects, including cats, dogs, and potted plants. Most of the images of people in the dataset are taken with handheld cameras, which is why this model doesn't recognize people in top-view cameras that well. So, the next step is to use a custom dataset of images taken from top-view cameras to create a more specialized model with better accuracy.

Train and Optimize Your Own Neural Network Model

This section is specifically for people detection from a top-view camera. Training a neural network for object detection can be a daunting task for a beginner, especially if you plan to deploy it to an embedded device, such as Raspberry Pi 4. For the purposes of this course, we use aXeleRate, a Keras-based framework for AI on the Edge (i.e., AI deployed to embedded devices). See Figure 2-11.

Figure 2-11. *aXeleRate logo*

aXeleRate allows for an easy, streamlined training and conversion process, where the user simply needs to add the data and configuration on the one end and receives a trained model, already converted to the target platform, on the other end. aXeleRate can be run in Google Colab, an interactive Jupyter Notebook service by Google, or on a local machine. Use the local machine-training option if you have an NVIDIA GPU and native installation of Ubuntu 18.04 or 20.04. Otherwise, it is recommended to use Google Colab, since it comes with all the required packages. Also, at the time of this writing, Google provides a certain amount of GPU hours for free accounts.

You can find the dataset in the materials for this book. It has the following folder structure:

- `imgs` contains training images
- `anns` contains training annotations in Pascal VOC format
- `imgs_validation` contains validation images
- `anns_validation` contains validation annotations in Pascal VOC format

The training and validation dataset comes primarily from three sources:

- Synthetic images generated with NVIDIA Isaac SDK
- Images converted from PIROPO database videos
- Personal recordings of the author converted to images

If you want to use your own dataset or add some samples to the existing one, you can use any object-detection dataset-annotation tool available, as long as it supports exporting to the Pascal VOC format.

For training in the Colab notebook, use Visual Studio Code to open the aXeleRate_people_topview.ipynb file in the Chapter_2/training folder, click Open in Colab, and follow the instructions in the notebook.

For local training, on your Ubuntu 18.04 (or 20.04) PC, install the Anaconda virtual environment manager and create a new environment:

```
conda create -n ml python=3.8
```

Then activate it with this command:

```
conda activate ml
```

Install the CUDA toolkit and NVIDIA packages for GPU-enabled training with this command:

```
conda install tensorflow-gpu~=2.4
```

And finally install aXeleRate in the environment with pip:

```
git clone https://github.com/AIWintermuteAI/aXeleRate.git
pip install -e .
```

Place the Chapter_2/training/people_topview.json file inside the configs folder in the aXeleRate repository. Change the path to the training and validation image/annotation folders in the .json config file and then run the following command to start the training (see Figure 2-12):

```
python axelerate/train.py --config configs/people_topview.json
```

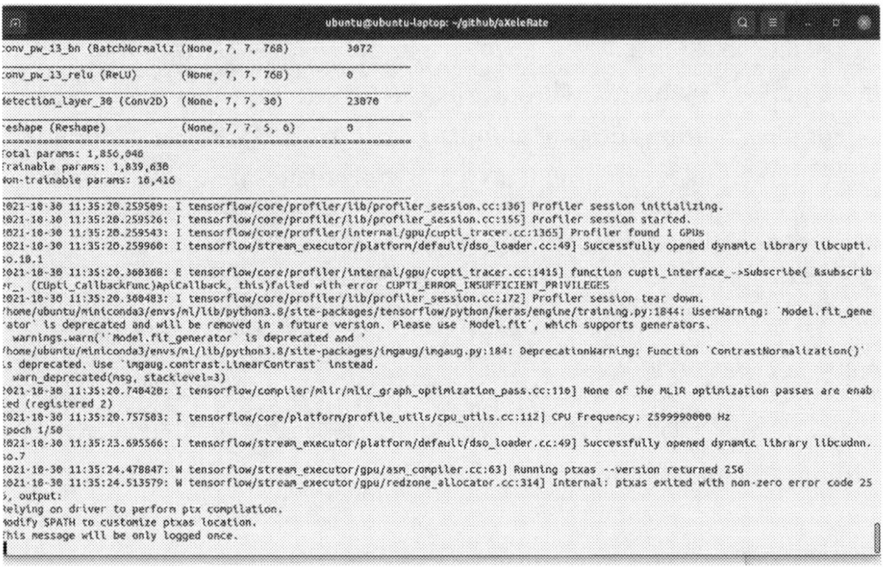

Figure 2-12. *Local training on Ubuntu 20.04 PC with NVIDIA GPU*

After training is completed, you can see the trained model in the projects/people_topview/[time-of-training-session] directory. Copy the resulting model file (with the .tflite extension) to the Chapter_2/models/ folder.

The commands used to launch an inference with the new model are similar to the ones you used to launch the inference with the pretrained model. From the Exercise_2 folder, run these commands:

```
python3 detector_video.py --model models/YOLO_best_mAP.
tflite --labels models/labels.txt --source file --file ../
video_samples/example_01.mp4
```

You will notice that there is less flickering of the bounding boxes, which means the model is better at detecting people from top-view footage. However, if you use a web camera or Pi camera and point it at the room, you might notice that the model you trained outputs a lot of false detections. This is expected, since the model is only trained to detect people from a top-view camera and will not perform well when presented with an entirely new view perspective. See Figure 2-13.

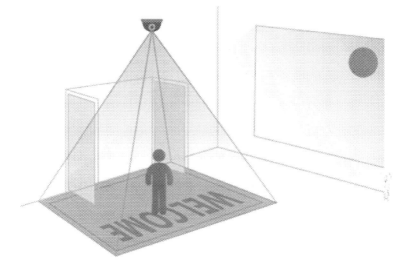

Figure 2-13. *The proper camera positioning for top-view people counting camera device*

For best results, mount Raspberry Pi 4 and the camera at the ceiling above the door frame or walkway, approximately 3-4 meters (10-12 feet) from the floor. In the "Pro Tips" section, you'll find example scripts and ideas on how to add more functionality to the basic implementation.

Pro Tips

While this script can work in a simple scenario, where you have only a single camera and are willing to manually record the count at the end of each day, you will probably want to automate the process even more. You can do that by connecting each Pi instance to a local SQL database or a cloud-based database. For example, you can use the SQLite database management system to store the people count in a local filesystem. This will enable you to query the count for any day or for a list of days that you want. You can learn more about SQLite at its official website.

If you want to store the people count in the cloud, you can use a database service provided by a cloud provider or one that runs on your own server (like the one deployed in the previous section). You can schedule a script to run each day at a specific time and record the people count. The script can then push the data to the cloud or local database.

To take full advantage of Raspberry Pi 4 CPU performance, when using the 64-bit Raspberry Pi OS image, you also need a custom-built version of TensorFlow Lite with threading support and XNNPACK optimized delegate enabled. You can find this in the `Chapter_2/Pro-tips` folder. Install it with `pip3`.

Another thing you can contemplate if you are building a scalable solution is the board choice for the device. While the standard Raspberry Pi 4 is great for prototyping, thanks to its rich interface selection on the development board, it can become a disadvantage when deploying at scale. This is mostly because your device doesn't need four USB ports and a display port. If your device is going to be deployed in an uncluttered environment and can tolerate a higher false-positive rate, you can train a smaller model and then use the previous generation board, the Raspberry Pi 3A. This is a stripped-down version of Raspberry Pi 3B, having only one USB port. It costs only 25 USD. An alternative option is to use the Raspberry Pi Compute Module 4, although in that case you need to design and manufacture your own carrier board. We discuss compute module applications and board design in later chapters.

Summary

This chapter introduced and explained the concepts of computer vision and deep learning and demonstrated their application for people counting in retail facilities. You learned how to train your own neural network model for people detection from a top-view camera and then convert it and optimize it for deployment on your Raspberry Pi 4.

CHAPTER 3

Vending Machine

Problem Overview

Vending machines are great! They help selling goods when personnel is limited, for example at night or in remote, underserviced locations.

The first modern coin-operated vending machines were introduced in London, England in the early 1880s. They dispensed postcards. That machine was invented by Percival Everitt in 1883 and soon became a widespread feature at railway stations and post offices, dispensing envelopes, postcards, and notepaper. See Figure 3-1.

© Elaine Wu, Dmitry Maslov 2022
E. Wu and D. Maslov, *Raspberry Pi Retail Applications*,
https://doi.org/10.1007/978-1-4842-7951-9_3

Figure 3-1. *An early coin-operated vending machine*

Since then, vending machines have increased in complexity.
Nowadays, they are used to sell almost anything, from iced drinks
to underwear. According to a report by the Food and Agriculture
Organization of the United Nations (FAO), in 2012 there were about 60
million vending machines in the world. The top four countries in terms of
vending machines are Japan, China, United States, and Russia. The global
vending machine industry was worth $41 billion in 2014 and is expected to
reach $52 billion by 2019, with a CAGR of 4.4 percent.

There are several types of vending machines. The most common
ones are:

- Candy and snack vending machines

- Coffee vending machines

- Fuel vending machines

- Redemption vending machines

- Vending kiosk vending machines

And of course there are many more! See Figure 3-2.

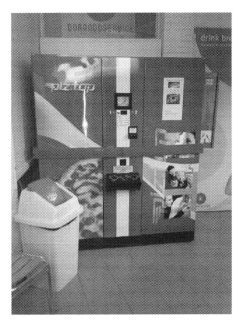

Figure 3-2. *A vending machine in Carpi, Italy that dispenses hot pizza*

As a business owner, you might need a specific type of vending machine or even a customized design. In this chapter, you learn how to use the Raspberry Pi Compute Module to process the orders and control the hardware of the machine. Furthermore, since the compute module cannot be used standalone without a carrier board, you learn how to interface the Raspberry Pi Compute Module with a customized carrier board for the specific hardware application.

Business Impact

As mentioned, vending machines can serve customers in times and locations where allocating full-time personnel is not economically viable. The main economic benefit of vending machines is their very low upkeep, especially as compared to human workers. The only things needed are electricity and regular maintenance/restocking services, thus they reduce labor costs in retail establishments. For example, a grocery store may want to have an employee restocking the shelves, but the cost of employing a worker is not justified by the extra revenue generated. Employing a vending machine allows the store to determine how much labor is needed to keep the shelves stocked.

Vending machines can also help a company have a more positive image with its customers and increase the coverage of its business. For example, a sandwich shop may want to offer delivery, but it would be too expensive to employ full-time delivery drivers. A vending machine could be placed in the lobby of the shop and the sandwiches could be delivered by a company that already delivers mail or packages.

Vending machines have the potential to increase employee productivity. Because cashiers are not needed, more registers can be opened without having to hire more employees. This leads to shorter lines and faster service.

Also, vending machines can provide a good level of privacy and security, as there is no direct human contact involved. This is especially true for coin-operated vending machines, as they don't have touchscreens or any other ways to identify the customer.

Seeing all the benefits vending machines can provide for retail businesses, you might be wondering if you can leverage Raspberry Pi 4 hardware to utilize this technology. The answer depends on the scale of your operations and the exact nature of services/products sold. Unlike with the project described in Chapter 2, creating/customizing a vending machine is a task only suitable for medium-to-large scale enterprises.

Smaller companies might find it is more cost-effective to use existing products. On the other hand, if your company sells a product that is not very well covered by existing options, building your own vending machine might make a lot of sense from an economic perspective. With Raspberry Pi 4 Compute Module as the hardware backbone, it is not too complicated to do so!

Related Knowledge

Vending machines rely on a number of different technologies to perform their functions. They typically use electricity to power the lights and the refrigeration. Some of the more advanced machines may use computerized systems that are capable of monitoring inventory levels and can ensure that the product is available when the customer wants it. Vending machines are a good example of the interplay between technology and business. The business requirements of a company will determine which technologies are best suited for that application.

Vending machines' mechanical systems differ drastically depending on the application, but their electronic components are similar. In general, a modern vending machine needs:

- A screen to interact with customers

- A computer to process requests and receive payments

- A controller for the mechanical system

Optional components include:

- A card reader for accepting purchases with plastic cards

- A WiFi/4G module for Internet connection

- A stock-monitoring system, such as one using computer vision

The regular Raspberry Pi 4 has too many unnecessary components that won't be useful for this application, such as USB ports, Ethernet ports, and HDMI connectors. On the other hand, it lacks a touchscreen and for mechanical systems control, an extension board must be used. All of that makes it impractical to use the standalone Raspberry Pi 4 board. Fortunately, there is a better solution—the Raspberry Pi 4 Compute Module (hereinafter referred to as Raspberry Pi 4 CM for brevity). It has a compact form factor for deeply embedded applications.

Raspberry Pi 4 CM incorporates a quad-core ARM Cortex-A72 processor, dual video output, and a wide selection of other interfaces. It contains many of the same specifications as the original Raspberry Pi 4, but it does away with most of the connectors, opting for a couple of 100-pin, high-density Hirose connectors on the underside. Rather than be an affordable desktop placement like the traditional Raspberry Pi, the Raspberry Pi 4 CM is intended for industrial applications where the module is embedded into a custom PCB and enclosure. It is available in 32 variants, with a range of RAM and eMMC Flash options, and with or without wireless connectivity. See Figure 3-3.

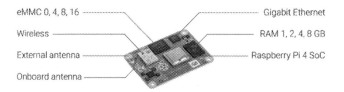

Figure 3-3. *A hardware overview of the Raspberry Pi 4 Compute Module*

Unlike a standalone Raspberry Pi 4 board, the Raspberry Pi 4 CM cannot be used without a carrier board, since it lacks IO interfaces. There is an CM4IO official carrier board for the Raspberry Pi 4 CM, which contains most of the inputs and outputs of the standard Raspberry Pi 4 and some more. See Figure 3-4.

Figure 3-4. *Reference carrier board for the Raspberry Pi 4 CM*

As you probably have guessed, the reference carrier board is not meant to be used in production. Instead, since the designs and schematics for it are freely available from the official Raspberry Pi source, it is meant to serve as a reference for people building their own carrier boards. Additionally, a handful of other hardware manufacturers offer carrier boards tailored for different applications. For example, the Dual Gigabit Ethernet carrier board for Raspberry Pi CM4 from Seeed Studio offers plentiful wired/wireless connectivity options in a compact form factor. These are especially suitable for designing/implementing router/NAS/ Internet-connected smart camera solutions. See Figure 3-5.

Figure 3-5. *Seeed Studio's Dual Gigabit Ethernet carrier board*

Or, the Gumstix Raspberry Pi CM4 PoE smart camera—which contains a Google Edge TPU ML Inference accelerator, camera connector, and a PoE-enabled Ethernet port—is ideal for smart, compact camera uses. See Figure 3-6.

Figure 3-6. *Gumstix Raspberry Pi CM4 PoE smart camera*

There are dozens of carrier boards available at the moment of writing this book and this list will only expand in the future.

If you decide to pick a readily available carrier board, pay attention to the following specifications:

- Display/touchscreen connector
- I2C/SPI/UART interfaces
- LTE module integration/support
- RTC (real-time clock) module and battery for it

If there is no board on the market that completely satisfies your product requirements, designing one is not a difficult task. Since this book focuses on use case analysis and software layer examples, we don't providing a complete step-by-step guide to designing a carrier board. Instead, we walk you through the important details and know-hows of the process, so that you know how to explain your requirements to the board designer.

Decide on PCB Manufacturer Beforehand

Different PCB manufacturers have different rules on board designs and what each manufacturer is capable of doing. So ideally you'll want to decide on a PCB manufacturer before you start designing the board or give the requirements to the third-party designer. Well-known PCB manufacturers include OSHPARK from the United States (see Figure 3-7), PCB TRAIN from the UK, and Seeed Studio's Fusion service from PRC.

Figure 3-7. *Logo of OSHPARK, a prominent PCB manufacturer*

Of course, there are many more. Very likely, your designer—be it a freelancer specialist or a company—has contacts with the PCB manufacturing service their clients use most often.

Determine the Interfaces You Need

Prototyping a PCB can be a time-consuming process, especially if you ship the PCB or PCBA from manufacturing facilities overseas. So it is very important to decide what elements you need on the carrier board and create a working prototype, which includes the hardware and software, to make sure you're not missing anything in the requirements to the carrier board design. With a working prototype, it is also easier to present the project to the PCB designer.

Look at Third-Party Open Source Designs for Your elements

In the open source world, there are many community-created designs, which you might find applicable to your project. Some of them are very advanced and you can use them with little or even no modification. See Figure 3-8.

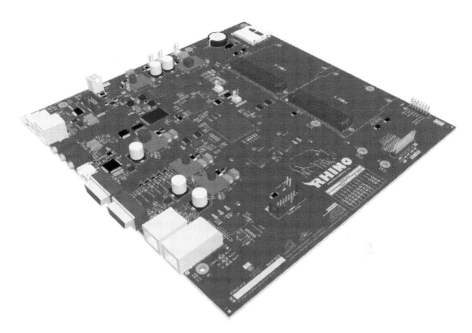

Figure 3-8. *RHINO, Reconfigurable Hardware Interface for Computing and Radio, is a relatively large platform for developing software-defined radio applications*

If you're building a consumer electronics device, you look at the Open Source Hardware page on the Element 14 community.

Look at How Other People Have Solved the Same Problem

At the very least, you might get some inspiration from what others have done before you. This is especially helpful if you have a very specific problem and there are no open source projects addressing this issue directly. OSHPARK has a great page with various open source projects for PCB designs.

Decide on Your Form Factor

Another very important decision is to decide what form factor to use for the carrier board, i.e. what will be the dimensions of the carrier board and how it will fit into the vending machine. If you plan to use a touchscreen for customer interaction, you should also keep that in mind when designing a board, so that the screen can be integrated with the carrier board for easier maintenance.

Determine the Location of Connectors and Headers

There are many different ways to place elements on the carrier board. You can put them on the front panel, on both sides of the board, or even under the board. It is very important to think about how you will place these elements and make sure you won't be blocking any connectors or headers with other elements.

Take Special Care of Heatsinks and Cooling Elements

A lot of Raspberry Pi 4 Compute Module interfaces are very close to each other, especially to the CPU. You need to make sure that there is enough space around Broadcom BCM2711 SoC and even more space around the connectors, like the HDMI and USB ports. See Figure 3-9.

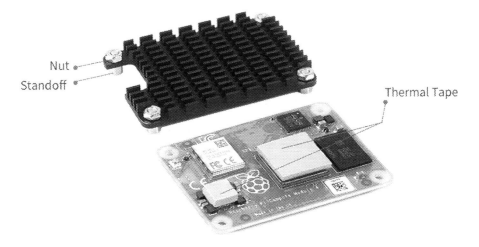

Figure 3-9. A heatsink for Raspberry Pi 4 CM

The last thing you want is a thermal runaway because of insufficient cooling while operating or an overheat while soldering the board, which is even more dangerous.

Implementation

For this chapter's project, you're going to implement a minimal prototype of a vending machine that can be controlled with a web interface displayed on the user's phone. This interface can be accessed by scanning a QR code on the vending machine. You'll also use a servo motor to push imaginary wares to your customers.

1) Implement servo control with Raspberry Pi 4.

2) Implement a simple web server that can be accessed on a local network and can be used to "buy" things from the vending machine.

3) Add a PayPal payment processor.

Implement Servo Control with Raspberry Pi 4

Servos typically have three inputs, two of which supply power to the motor located inside the plastic body. The third input controls how much the servo turns. See Figure 3-10.

Figure 3-10. *Very common 9g micro-servo from TowerPro*

Usually, the input signal is pulse-width modulated (PWM) and its frequency doesn't change over time. Instead, the servo motor rotates to a certain angle when the duty cycle of the PWM input signal changes. The servo used in this example can turn 180 degrees in total (90 degrees in each direction). When the duty cycle is 5% (a one-millisecond long, high pulse), the servo rotates to its minimum position. If the duty cycle changes to 10% (which is a two-millisecond long, high pulse), the servo rotates all the way to the right. Duty cycles in between correlate to different angles between -90° and +90°. However, these numbers might vary for different servos and between manufacturers. Therefore, it's always necessary to consult the datasheet of the servo.

Note that the Raspberry Pi shouldn't supply the voltage to the servo. Instead, employ an external power supply to drive the servo motor, because the Raspberry Pi's GPIO pins might be unable to supply enough power to make the motor turn at an acceptable rate.

To make a Raspberry Pi control a servo motor, connect the +5 V and GND lines of the servo to an external power supply and the remaining signal wire to any I/O pin of the Raspberry Pi. See Figure 3-11.

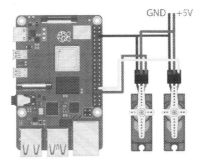

Figure 3-11. *Connection schematic for Raspberry Pi 4 and two servos*

Don't forget to connect any GND pin of the Raspberry Pi to the ground of the power supply as well.

As mentioned, servos typically expect a PWM signal that tells them where to turn. Therefore, there are several methods to rotate a servo to a specific angle. One method is to use the gpiozero library that contains a servo module.

You can use 64-bit image of Raspberry Pi OS as a starting point, the same one you flashed on the SD card in Chapter 2.

You can use pip to install the library on a Raspberry Pi. If the rpi. gpio package isn't installed, download it as well. Otherwise, the gpiozero library won't work:

```
sudo apt-get install python3-rpi.gpio
pip3 install gpiozero
```

Then, from the `Chapter_3` folder, execute the following command to install the rest of the dependencies necessary to run the other examples:

```
pip3 install -r requirements.txt
```

Once that's done, it's possible to execute the following script with Python3 (`Chapter_3/exercise_1/test_servo.py`):

```python
from gpiozero import Servo
from time import sleep

servo = Servo(25)
try:
        while True:
        servo.min()
        sleep(0.5)
        servo.mid()
        sleep(0.5)
        servo.max()
        sleep(0.5)
except KeyboardInterrupt:
        print("Program stopped")
```

As you can see, this library allows you to quickly turn the servo to one of three predefined positions. This simple Python script first imports the required libraries. Then, it defines that the servo is connected to pin 25 before starting an infinite loop in which the servo gets rotated to its minimum, mid, and maximum positions. In between angle changes, the script waits for half a second. See Figure 3-12.

Figure 3-12. *A 9g servo connected to Raspberry Pi 4*

Since servos are essentially just DC motors with a potentiometer and a control chip that allows them to turn to a certain angle, you can instruct the servo to turn to a precise angle with the help of the AngularServo class in the gpiozero library.

Use the following code to create an AngularServo class object and let the servo rotate its shaft slowly from 0 (initial position) to 180 (the maximum position). You can find the following script at Chapter_3/exercise_1/test_servo_precise.py:

```python
from gpiozero import AngularServo
import time

s = AngularServo(17, min_angle=0, max_angle=180)

try:
    for i in range(180):
        s.angle = i
        time.sleep(0.1)
except KeyboardInterrupt:
    print("Program stopped")
```

As mentioned in the documentation for the gpiozero library, to reduce servo jitter, use the pigpio pin driver rather than the default RPi.GPIO driver (pigpio uses DMA sampling for much more precise edge timing). You can use the pigpio pin driver by adding the following lines to the beginning of the script:

```
from gpiozero.pins.native import NativeFactory
from gpiozero import Device, LED
Device.pin_factory = NativeFactory()
```

Now that you know how to control a servo, it is time to work on the second element of the vending machine—user interaction.

Implement a Simple Web Server with Flask

In order to create the web server, you will be using a Python microframework called Flask. Flask is a web framework. It's a Python module that lets you easily develop web applications. It has a small and easy-to-extend core and allows for implementing features like URL routing and template engine. It's easy to get started with Flask, because it doesn't have a huge learning curve.

On top of that, it's very explicit, which increases readability. To create the "Hello World" app, you only need a few lines of code.

This is a boilerplate code example.

```
from flask import Flask
app = Flask(__name__)

@app.route('/')
def hello_world():
    return 'Hello World!'

if __name__ == '__main__':
    app.run()
```

If you want to develop on your local computer, you can do so easily. Save this program as server.py and run it with python server.py.

```
python server.py
 * Serving Flask app "hello"
 * Running on http://127.0.0.1:5000/ (Press CTRL+C to quit)
```

It then starts a web server that's available only on your computer. In a web browser, open localhost on port 5000 (the URL) and you'll see "Hello World" show up.

You can see the example code for the vending machine interface in the Chapter_3/exercise_2 folder. Let's go through the most important parts of the code.

```
qrcode = pyqrcode.create('http://' + get_ip()+ ':5000')
print(qrcode.terminal(quiet_zone=1))
```

This creates a QR code using a dedicated library called pyqrcode. The QR code contains the IP address and the port of the server and prints this out in the terminal. You then use your phone's camera to scan that code and visit a web page that contains a vending machine control interface.

```
app = Flask(__name__)
app.run(host='0.0.0.0', port=5000, debug=True)
```

These two lines are responsible for creating the Flask web server.

You then use the route() decorator to tell Flask what URL should trigger the function. The vending machine interface will have the following pages:

```
@app.route("/")
```

This is the main page, which will contain items, their prices, and the buttons to purchase an item.

```
@app.route("/<item>/<action>")
```

This route will get the item name and action ("buy") from the user's browser when the user clicks an item button. In the sample app, it will redirect the user to the success page.

```
@app.route("/success")
@app.route("/cancel")
```

These two routes display a payment success or failure message. The success route function will also trigger servo movement, which is supposed to push the goods the customer purchased out of the shelf.

It stores the items' names, prices, and availability status in a dictionary as follows:

```
item_dict = {'coke': {'price':1, 'available': True},
'energy bar': {'price':2.5, 'available': True},
'chewing gum': {'price':0.5, 'available': True}}
```

Then, when the main page is visited, the program passes the values from this dictionary to the .html template:

```
templateData = {
'items' : item_dict
}
return render_template('main.html', **templateData)
```

Let's look at the contents of the main.html file located in the templates folder. This is a Jinja template and it resembles Python code. For example

```
{% for item in items %}
```

This line loops through the values in the items entry and renders the following elements for each item:

```
<h2>{{ item }}
```

```
{% if items[item].available == true %}
```

```
<strong>{{ items[item].price}} USD</strong></h2><div
class="row"><div class="col-md-2">
<a href="/{{item}}/buy" class="btn btn-block btn-lg btn-
default" role="button">Buy</a></div></div>
{% else %}
<strong>{{ items[item].price}} USD </strong></h2><div
class="row"><div class="col-md-2">
<a href="/{{item}}/buy" class="btn btn-block btn-lg btn-
primary" role="button">Not available</a></div></div>
{% endif %}
{% endfor %}
```

This template block writes the name of the item in bold and then, depending on if the item's `available` value is `true` or not, displays "Buy" or "Not available" on the button. Pressing the button will cause the browser to visit the /name-of-the-item/buy route (e.g., /cola/buy).

```
@app.route("/<item>/<action>")
def action(item, action):
    global hostname

    print(item, item_dict[item]['price'])
    return redirect(hostname + "/success", code=302)
```

Which in turn will call an action function, which prints the name and price of the item and redirects the user to the /success route of the web server.

```
@app.route("/success")
def success():
    global hostname
    control_servo('servo.min')
    return render_template('success.html')
```

The /success route of the server sends the servo to its minimum angle and renders the success.html template with very simple content.

```
<body>
<h1>Vedi Vending</h1>
<h2>Order successful</h2>
Please take your purchase!
<meta http-equiv="refresh" content="10; URL=/" />

</body>
</html>
```

The <meta http-equiv="refresh" content="10; URL=/" /> command will cause the user's browser to automatically go back to the server's main page after ten seconds.

You can run the application from the Chapter_3/exercise_2 folder by typing the following in the terminal:

```
python3 app.py
```

It will display a QR code, which you need to scan with your phone's camera application. For this example your phone needs to be on the same network as the Raspberry Pi. See Figure 3-13.

Figure 3-13. *An interface that can be seen from a mobile phone browser after scanning the QR code*

We discuss how to implement a more scalable variant in the "Pro Tips" section of this chapter.

You can now make "purchases" from the vending machine with your phone.

Of course, unless you're going to create a charity vending machine, you want to add a payment option to the device. See Figure 3-14.

Figure 3-14. *PayPal Checkout SDK usage*

For illustrative purposes, we're going to use the PayPal payment SDK here, since PayPal is a globally available payment system. Your actual solution might handle the notes, tokens, or even cryptocurrency!

Add a PayPal Payment Processor

To get started with processing PayPal payments, you need to download and install the latest version of PayPal Python SDK. If you installed Python3 libraries from the `requirements.txt` file in the `Chapter_3` folder, you should already have PayPal Python SDK installed.

After making sure PayPal Python SDK is present, check the sample application code in the `Chapter_3/exercise_3` folder. It is very similar to the Exercise 2 code, with a few differences. First of all, there is a new file called `create_order.py`, which takes care of creating an order request with the name and price of the item. You need to import the `create_order` function from the `CreateOrder` module in `app.py`. The most important difference in the `app.py` file is that, instead of simply redirecting to the `success.html` page, it creates a PayPal order with the name and price of the item and then redirects to the PayPal payment page.

```
response = CreateOrder().create_order(item_dict[item]['price'],
item, hostname)
order_id = ''
print('Creating Order...')
if response.status_code == 201:
    order_id = response.result.id
for link in response.result.links:
    print(('\t{} link: {}\tCall Type: {}'.format(str(link.rel)
    .capitalize(), link.href, link.method)))
    print('Created Successfully\n')
    print('Copy approve link and paste it in browser. Login with
    buyer account and follow the instructions.\nOnce approved
    hit enter...')
    return redirect(response.result.links[1].href, code=302)
else:
    print('Link is unreachable')
    exit(1)
```

In order for this example to work, you need to specify two environment variables in a bash shell before you run app.py:

PAYPAL_CLIENT_ID

   and

PAYPAL_CLIENT_SECRET.

You can get these variables by going to the PayPal Developers Website home page at https://developer.paypal.com/home . Then click Login to the Dashboard. Go to [Your Name], then go to Dashboard in the top-right corner. Choose the Create App button. See Figure 3-15.

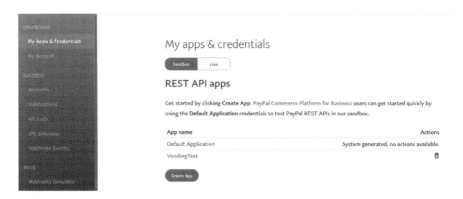

Figure 3-15. *PayPal app creation interface in the dashboard*

Fill in the details for the new app and then create it. A new screen will open. On the next page, you can see your PayPal client ID and secret.

Note   You will find the sandbox app settings and credentials on the same page.

To set PAYPAL_CLIENT_ID and PAYPAL_CLIENT_SECRET in a bash terminal session, execute the following commands:

```
export PAYPAL_CLIENT_ID="your-Paypal-client-id"
export PAYPAL_CLIENT_SECRET="your-Paypal-secret"
```

Note   Environmental variables do not persist between sessions, so you need to set them up if you open another terminal. Alternatively you can add these variables permanently to a .bashrc file on your Raspberry Pi 4. Needless to say, that solution only works during development and not for actual production, because of the security risks associated with storing CLIENT_ID and PASSWORD in an unencrypted file.

After that, type the following in the terminal:

```
python3 app.py
```

This is where you executed previous commands to test the app. See Figure 3-16.

Figure 3-16. *The result of clicking one of the items on the web page from Figure 3-13*

You'll see a familiar web interface from Exercise 2. The difference this time is that when you click the item, you'll be redirected to a PayPal sandbox payment page (see Figure 3-17). From there, you can pay with a mock account. If the mock payment is successful, you'll be redirected to the /success route of your web server, which will display the corresponding web page and cause the servo to go to its minimum position.

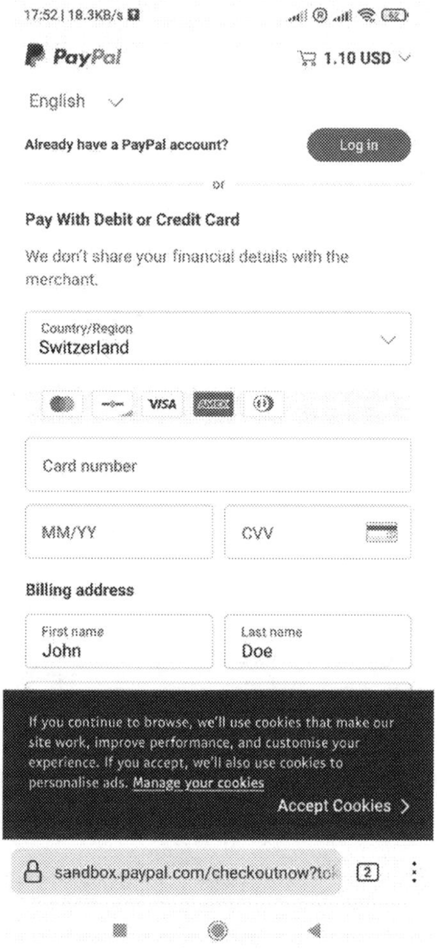

Figure 3-17. *PayPal mobile Checkout page*

Pro Tips

While this implementation can be done on a small scale (say, a dozen vending machines), for large-scale deployment, a centralized server is better in terms of stability and security. Customers would be directed to this centralized server upon scanning the QR code. The link in the QR code in this scenario would contain each vending machine's unique ID. The central server would query the vending machines for supply status of items and, once the payment is successfully completed, it would send the signal to the particular vending machine to move the servo. See Figure 3-18.

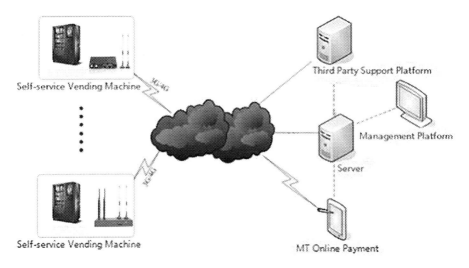

Figure 3-18. *A possible schematic for implementing a production-ready vending machine payment system*

The difficulty of implementing the central server approach depends on how many machines are involved and how geographically distant they are from the main server. In the case of a dozen vending machines in a local area, a central server can be implemented using a Raspberry Pi or a low-end computer along with a touchscreen. In the case of a larger-scale project, a server farm will be required. Another consideration is the time required for each vending machine to receive the signal from the server. A vending machine on the other side of the globe may take a while to receive the signal from the server. In order to reduce latency, a local server can be implemented on top of the central server.

The system can be upgraded to support multiple levels of security, from a simple PIN code to fingerprint recognition. It can also be extended to include other products, such as newspapers, lottery tickets, and food. Other types of vending machines could also be created, such as snack vending machines, drink vending machines, and ice cream vending machines, all of which require more operations. Additional elements, such as a bio-sensor to measure the temperature of the cold storage to prevent the food from going bad, could be added in the framework described in the chapter.

Summary

In this chapter, you learned how to utilize the Raspberry Pi 4 development board or compute module to build a customized prototype vending machine. Among the technologies discussed in this chapter were:

- Important points to pay attention to when creating a customized carrier board

- How to use the Python Flask framework to build a web application

- How to use the PayPal Checkout SDK to provide a payment gateway for vending machine purchases

CHAPTER 4

Interactive Touchscreen Directory

Problem Overview

Digital directories provide valuable ways to help customers find shops, businesses, office locations, and even specific individuals. In fact, digital directories have become so common in retail, communication, and facility businesses that consumers often expect them to be provided on demand, whether they are going to the airport, a shopping mall, or a hospital campus. See Figure 4-1.

E. Wu and D. Maslov, *Raspberry Pi Retail Applications*,
https://doi.org/10.1007/978-1-4842-7951-9_4

Figure 4-1. *A touchscreen directory at a shopping mall*

In addition to location data and map listings, digital catalogs can also provide local information, including weather, transportation options, and digital advertisements. The most advanced directories can even send map data to mobile phones.

Interactive digital media help retail businesses interact better with and help their customers. Most retailers have begun to use touchscreen, retail, digital signage solutions and creative interactive content to attract customers and improve their in-store experiences. This includes using interactive mirrors, videos, touchscreens, and more. It can be cost effective and easy to set up a robust interactive digital solution with a credit card-sized SBC, such as Raspberry Pi.

You can use touchscreen navigation solutions to help your visitors and customers easily navigate your store. You can design the most advanced digital signage path-finding solution on a very small budget using Raspberry Pi. Furthermore, you can remotely update directory information. Interactive way-finding maps provide three-dimensional navigation to help customers locate events, promotions, businesses, or other destinations at your facility.

Business Impact

Interactive directories and mobile robots with touchscreens are changing the way retail stores advertise and help customers. Way-finding touchscreen signage enables the retail industry to create a more efficient shopping experience by meticulously drawing a map of a mall. Through interactive experiences, retail screens can modernize the store's image and create a lasting, positive experience. The most important thing is to provide customers with the most convenient and immediate way to obtain the information they are looking for in a mall or store.

Traditionally, visitors may have used a printed brochure of a shopping mall map to guide them. However, a one-page flyer cannot include everything you want to reach out to every customer. An interactive touchscreen-enabled directory—or perhaps even a mobile directory robot—can provide guidance to customers and promotion opportunities to retailers.

By simply using a single-board Human Machine Interface (HMI), you can easily promote in-store offers, display current information about events, and deliver other important messages to customers. With Raspberry Pi-based interactive devices integrated with a touchscreen and customized using dashboard software, retailers can display all kinds of mall activities. You can design a multitude of scenarios to meet customers' shopping demands in different areas of your store, help them find the right routes, and reach them with advertisements.

There are various opportunities for promotion:

- Interactive maps with routes
- Best sales catalogs

- Facilities

- Upcoming promotions

- Event calendars

For example, you can build a directory screen to show the different stores available in the mall or you can build a directory to show which items are in stock at each register. This type of directory is very helpful to shoppers, especially when they are looking for something specific. See Figure 4-2.

Figure 4-2. *A touchscreen directory being used for indoor navigation*

A touchscreen directory allows shoppers to find information about outlets and amenities and allows business owners to advertise special promotions in order to attract more customers.

A touchscreen directory embedded with a Raspberry Pi can be installed anywhere. You can set it up in the lobby of the mall or you can install it at the entrance of your shop. It can also be used for internal purposes if you are looking for a simple directory to guide employees through your offices. You can display anything you like on this directory, such as information about holidays, employee contact details, or anything else that is important to you and your company. Raspberry Pi has many applications in retail environments because it is small and inexpensive, yet versatile enough to handle all kinds of tasks that come your way. This chapter provides a step-by-step guide to building a touchscreen directory using a Raspberry Pi-powered HMI device with a high-resolution touchscreen display.

Related Knowledge

In this scenario, Raspberry Pi is playing the role of the Human Machine Interface (HMI). HMIs are devices that allow humans to interact with machine systems. These devices work by sending and receiving signals that can be read by humans and machines. HMI devices can be as simple as a light that flashes when some event occurs or more complex, like a device that is used to control industrial processes. See Figure 4-3.

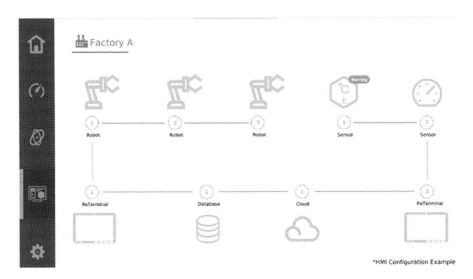

Figure 4-3. *An example of HMI device interface*

HMIs, also known as user interfaces (UIs) or operator interface terminals (OITs), include hardware and software solutions. They are used between systems/machines and human operators to exchange information and communication. HMIs can handle the control, management, and/or visualization of equipment processes, ranging from simple touchscreen inputs to control panels of highly complex industrial automation systems.

HMIs come in various form factors, from built-in screens on machines, to panel PCs, to tablets, but no matter what their format or the terminology you use, their purpose is to provide information on mechanical performance and progress.

Let's look at Seeed Studio's reTerminal as an example, powered by the Raspberry Pi 4 Computer Module with 4GB RAM and 32GB eMMC. It is a sturdy, reliable HMI device that can easily and efficiently work with IoT and cloud systems to unlock endless scenarios at the edge. See Figure 4-4.

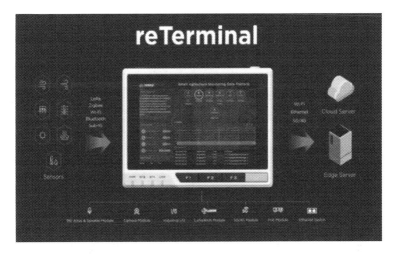

Figure 4-4. *reTerminal, a Raspberry Pi 4 CM carrier board with a touchscreen and built-in sensors*

In an industrial environment, HMIs play a key role. In the context of increasing digitization, HMIs have become irreplaceable as a control plane for industrial operations and equipment of various scales.

For example, factory operators can use HMIs to monitor, manage, and control autonomous machines and production lines. On the other hand, HMIs have become an important part of the operability of the system. They can control field-deployed equipment that may not be physically reachable, such as in large-scale, remote IoT.

In order to create a shopping directory UI that can be run on a Raspberry Pi, you need to choose a suitable Python GUI (graphical user interface) framework tool. As an interactive programming language, Python is currently leading the trend (*Top Computer Languages 2021:* StatisticsTimes.com) and is relatively easy to use. Starting to write a GUI framework is not a difficult task.

Python has been the leading programming language among five countries: the United States, India, Germany, the United Kingdom, and France, which surpasses the second highest usage of Java. Python's usage is more than double that of Java in Germany, the United Kingdom, and France.

Python provides multiple choices, such as PyQt, Tkinter (see Figure 4-5), wxPython, PySimpleGUI, and PyGTK, for GUI frameworks on different platforms (Windows, Linux, and Mac).

Figure 4-5. *The Tkinter logo*

For this chapter's project, a digital shopping directory deployed into reTerminal, we use Tkinter as the GUI framework.

Tkinter is a Python-binding package for the Tk GUI toolkit, built with the standards of the Python interface of the Tk GUI toolkit and the GUI toolkit of Python. Tkinter includes Python's standard libraries for Linux, Microsoft Windows, and macOS X.

The tkinter package (the Tk interface) is the standard Python interface to the Tk GUI toolkit. Since Tkinter is built into the Python installation package, you can import the Tkinter library after installing Python. For the purposes of simplifying the interface development, we utilize PAGE, a GUI generator, to create the layout and populate it with different widgets. PAGE is a cross-platform drag-and-drop GUI generator.

It allows users to easily build a Python GUI window containing a series of Tk and ttk widgets. PAGE is derived from Virtual Tcl, forked to generate Python modules to implement the desired GUI.

Implementation

In this section, we cover:

1) Basic Tkinter usage.

2) Build an interface with the PAGE GUI generator.

3) Deploy it into the Raspberry Pi

This section walks you through the development of a touchscreen-based application for the Raspberry Pi and the use of the Tkinter module in Python. The main purpose of this project is to demonstrate how to build user interfaces using Python and Tkinter. The main advantage of using Tkinter is its simplicity and ease of use. At the end of this project, you will have built a simple directory system that can be used on a touchscreen for the Raspberry Pi.

Basic Tkinter Usage

You can find the following code in the Chapter_4/exercise_1 folder.

The first step in this project is to start Python and load the Tkinter module:

```
import tkinter as tk
```

This imports the module and makes it available for use. Next, create a Tkinter window:

```
win = tk.Tk()
```

This creates a blank window that can be used to draw objects. The next step is to add a few options to the window:

```
win.resizable(width=False, height=False) # Disallow resizing
of window
win.title('Tkinter Hello World Demo') # Set title bar text
```

With these options set, you can start drawing on the window:

```
win.title('Tkinter Hello World Demo') # Set title bar text
win.geometry('320x240') # Set window size
```

The next step is to add some objects to the windows:

```
Label = tk.Label(win, text='Hello Tkinter',
bg='blue', fg='white',
relief='raised', anchor='nw').place(x = 100, y = 60)

Button = tk.Button(win, command=win.quit, text='Quit',
bg='orange', width=10).place(x = 100, y = 100)
```

The Label object allows you to draw text on the screen. The parameters are self-explanatory, with the exception of the anchor parameter, which determines where the text will appear. The Button object allows you to draw a button on the screen that can be clicked. The quit command is called when the button is clicked. Finally, you need to add an event handler for when the Quit button is clicked:

```
win.bind('<Button-1>', win.quit)  # This registers the Quit
handler to the button <Button-1>
```

This registers an event handler when the user clicks the button. We use the win.quit function to close the window, which ensures that the program stops. The final step is to start the window.

```
win.mainloop()
```

When the window starts, it will show the Label and Button objects, as shown in Figure 4-6.

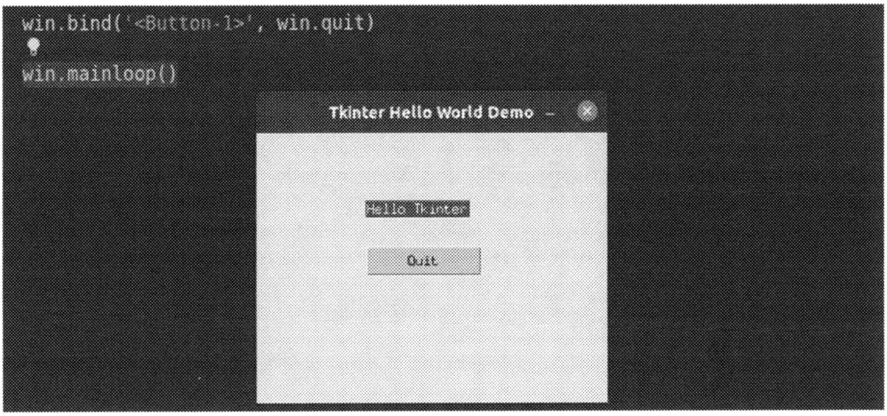

Figure 4-6. *Sample Tkinter app execution result*

You can now use the mouse or a touchscreen to click the button and close the window.

Build an Interface with the PAGE GUI Generator

Use the steps in the following sections to build the interface using the PAGE GUI generator.

Install PAGE GUI Generator

It's better to install the PAGE GUI generator and set up the preliminary design on your PC. Next are the instructions for installing and using PAGE on Ubuntu 20.04 Desktop.

Download page-6.2.tgz from https://sourceforge.net/projects/page/files/page/.

Place the page-6.2.tgz archive in the Chapter_4 directory and extract it with the following command (see Figure 4-7):

```
tar zxvf page-6.2.tgz
```

```
ⵏ    ubuntu@ubuntu-laptop: ~/github/Raspberry_PI_Book/Chapt...    Q  ≡   _  ▢  ✕
)age/examples/clone/
)age/examples/clone/called_support.py
)age/examples/clone/main.py
)age/examples/clone/called.py
)age/examples/clone/called.tcl
)age/examples/clone/README
)age/examples/clone/main_support.py
)age/examples/clone/main.tcl
)age/examples/canvas/
)age/examples/canvas/canvas.tcl
)age/examples/canvas/canvas.py
)age/examples/canvas/README
)age/examples/canvas/canvas_support.py
)age/examples/scrolledwindow/
)age/examples/scrolledwindow/new.py
)age/examples/scrolledwindow/f_support.py
)age/examples/scrolledwindow/new.tcl
)age/examples/scrolledwindow/new_support.py
)age/examples/scrolledwindow/f.tcl
)age/examples/scrolledwindow/f.py
)age/examples/scrolledwindow/pt-arena_hills.jpg
)age/examples/directory-tree.py
)age/page.py
(base) ubuntu@ubuntu-laptop:~/github/Raspberry_PI_Book/Chapter_4$ █
```

Figure 4-7. *PAGE files extracted to the Chapter_4/page folder*

This will put the whole distribution in the subdirectory called page. Run the `configure` script from the page folder.

```
./configure
```

If you want to use JPG images in PAGE, you need to install three additional packages using the following commands to insert JPG images:

```
sudo apt-get libtk-img python3-pil python3-pil.imagetk
```

Run this command in the folder you extracted the PAGE editor to:

```
./page
```

From the File menu, choose New to start new project-building interfaces. Save this to the exercise_2 folder in Chapter_4 under the name directory.tcl.

Create the UI with Tkinter Widgets in PAGE

Next, you are going to create an instance of tk.Label, insert the shopping mall map image into that label, create several buttons to pin at different locations, and finally add the corresponding message box to shops using another instance of tk.Label.

The first thing you should do is change the name of the main window. You can do that by editing the Alias and Title entries in the Attribute Editor. Set Alias to Directory and Title to Directory. Additionally, set the width to 1280 and the height to 720, and make them non-resizable.

Then, click Label in the Widget Toolbar and click an empty space in the Design window. After that, in the Attribute Editor on the right side of the screen, write "map" in the Alias field. Then choose the suitable image (an example map is provided in the Chapter_4/working_project/images folder) by clicking the three dots icon next to the image field. Set the label width to 1280 and the height to 720. See Figure 4-8.

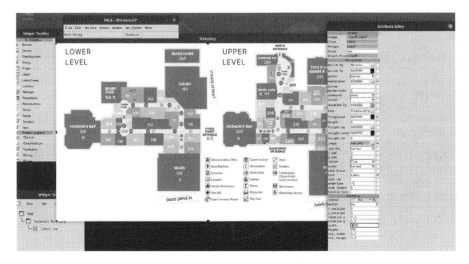

Figure 4-8. *Main window and map label with an image of the mall map set*

After you import the image, place three Button widgets at different locations. You can do that the same way that you placed the map label—by clicking the Button widget in the Widget Toolbar and then clicking the empty space in the window. See Figure 4-9.

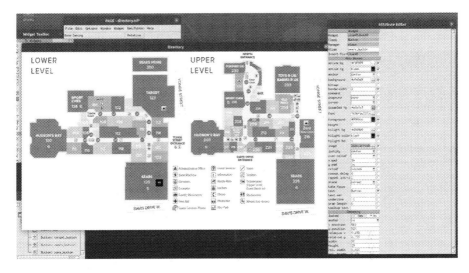

Figure 4-9. *Button position and attributes*

Note   If you get the You cannot insert a widget inside
a label! error message, it means you're trying to insert the
Button widget into the map label. Click the empty space in the
window instead. After the button is placed in the window, move
it to the desired position. Choose an icon for every button in the
Attribute Editor by clicking the three dots icon next to the image
field. Be sure to provide a meaningful alias for every button, such as
sears_button.

Finally, place a shop description. To do that, create a new label
and place it inside the Main window. Edit the alias to description_
label. Don't set the text yet, as you'll do that later, when you write the
program logic.

Note   You need to create only one label for the shop description.

Write Program Logic in Python

While you have several buttons, you only need one label, since you can move the label and change its text programmatically, depending on which button was pressed.

Generate the Python GUI from Tkinter. To do that, first choose Gen_Python ➤ Generate Support Module and then click Save in the newly opened window. Second, choose Gen_Python ➤ Generate Python GUI and then click Save in newly opened window. After that, you'll have two new files in the exercise_2 folder: directory.py and directory_support.py. See Figure 4-10.

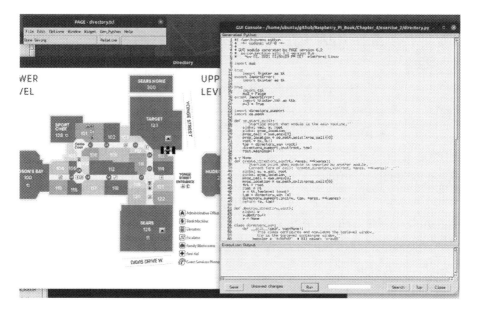

Figure 4-10. *Python 3 code export interface*

You can open the exported Python file in your favorite IDE (we recommend using Visual Studio Code) to write code logic about what will happen after the button is pressed. See Figure 4-11.

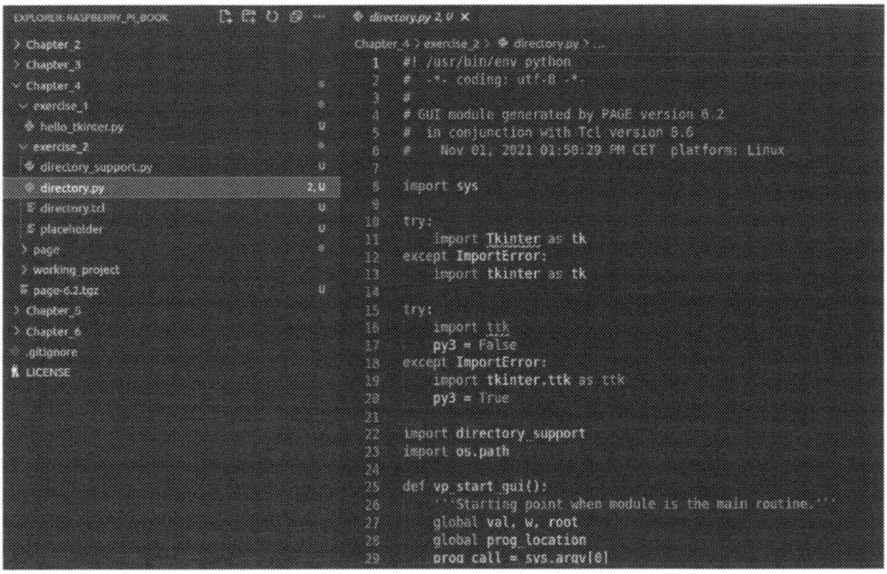

Figure 4-11. *Project structure in VS Code*

Add the show_label() method to the Directory class. That method is responsible for placing the label in a certain position and configuring the label text.

```
def show_label(self, text, x, y):
        self.Label2.place(relx=x, rely=y, height=100, width=200)
        self.Label2.configure(text=text)
```

Then add the btn_name_x, btn_name_y, and btn_name_txt variables to each of the buttons. Here is an example for zara_button (see Figure 4-12):

```
self.zara_button = tk.Button(top)
zara_txt = """Zara
Opening 9AM 10PM
Yonge St #17600
975-914-1580
Promotion items:"""
```

```
zara_btn_x = 0.914
zara_btn_y = 0.389

self.zara_button.place(relx=zara_btn_x, rely=zara_btn_y,
height=19, width=20)
self.zara_button.configure(activebackground="#f9f9f9")
self.zara_button.configure(borderwidth="2")
photo_location = os.path.join(prog_location,"../working_
project/images/icon_arrowbutton.gif")
global _img3
_img3 = tk.PhotoImage(file=photo_location)
self.zara_button.configure(image=_img3)
self.zara_button.configure(text='''Button''')
self.zara_button.configure(text='''Button''',
command = lambda: self.show_label(zara_txt, x = zara_btn_x -
0.05, y = zara_btn_y + 0.05))
```

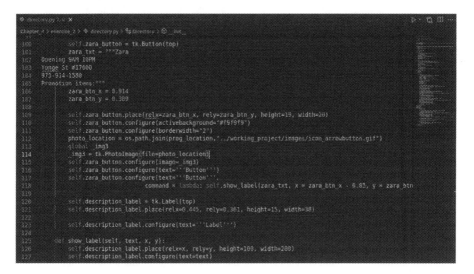

Figure 4-12. *Added show_label (method) and parameters for
zara_button*

The only change to make to other buttons are the x, y positions and the text that gets passed to the show_label() method of the Directory class, which was automatically generated by the PAGE GUI editor. You can see the full example in the Chapter_4/working_project folder. See Figure 4-13.

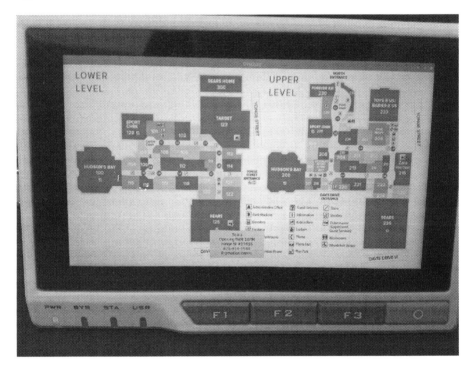

Figure 4-13. *Working project displayed on reTerminal*

You can run this by executing the following command from the project folder:

```
DISPLAY=:0 python3 directory.py
```

Pro Tips

What are some alternatives to the relatively simple interface offered by Tkinter? Other popular and much more flexible options for creating user interfaces with Python include PyQt and PySimpleGUI. They can be a bit more challenging to learn, but offer a lot of power and extensibility.

Qt for Python: Qt5.x Qt is a set of C++ libraries and tools for creating GUIs. PySide2 is an official binding of Qt5.x for Python. PySide2 also supports remote debugging with the Qt Creator IDE, as well as cross-platform deployment. See Figure 4-14.

Figure 4-14. *QT logo*

PySide2 and Qt5 are based on the Qt for Python project. There is strong compatibility between the two frameworks, making it nearly 99.9 percent of the same API. PySide2 and Qt5 provide powerful and simple features for Python developers. There are also abundant documentation and examples you can find in the developer community for both beginners and experts to use as examples when developing applications. Qt for Python is popular, with extensive community support and more than 1 million software developers.

PySimpleGUI (see Figure 4-15) was developed by Mike B in 2018, and it aims to make GUI programming easier for Python beginners. PySimpleGUI combines the features of several popular Python GUI frameworks (such as Qt and Tkinter) and provides standardized code examples to help beginners build Lego-style GUIs. Naturally, this means that even beginners can easily create beautiful and intuitive interfaces without having to delve into the complexity of framework functions!

Figure 4-15. *PySimpleGUI logo*

Summary

In the chapter, you learned how to transform Raspberry Pi 4 into an interactive directory to help mall customers or other retail environments. The chapter discussed the development of a touchscreen-based application for the Raspberry Pi, together with the usage of the Tkinter module in Python.

The main purpose of this project is to demonstrate how to build user interfaces using Python and Tkinter. The main advantage of using Tkinter is its simplicity and ease of use. At the end of this project, you will have built a simple directory system that can be used on a touchscreen for the Raspberry Pi. It can be run, for example, on the Seeed Studio reTerminal, a carrier board for Raspberry Pi 4 CM. We used the PAGE GUI generator to generate a UI for the directory and then translated it into a Python 3 project.

CHAPTER 5

Voice Interaction Drive-through Self-service Station

Problem Overview

Due to the rapid development of the artificial intelligence technology, a fast and reliable ASR (Automatic Speech Recognition) system finally became a reality. Neural network models capable of converting audible speech into written text for later parsing are now available to almost everyone on the globe, in hundreds of different languages. They are used in intelligent assistant services, such as Siri and Google Assistant, telephone customer services, and in many other fields. The next logical step is to move the dialogue with a customer from a mobile app to a voice-controlled device such as Amazon Echo or Google Home. See Figure 5-1.

© Elaine Wu, Dmitry Maslov 2022
E. Wu and D. Maslov, *Raspberry Pi Retail Applications*,
https://doi.org/10.1007/978-1-4842-7951-9_5

Figure 5-1. *Amazon smart speakers at an exhibition*

The possibility of using a self-service kiosk with voice control is another step closer to creating a "fully automated" fast food restaurant.

The problem of fast food restaurants is that, due to their high throughput, it is financially difficult to serve every customer by a human employee. That is why the industry is looking for solutions to automate the process of serving the order. Two of the main problems are the volume of orders and the payment process. The solution to the first problem is to use a self-service kiosk with a touchscreen interface. This is already in use in airports and railway stations, and it is a good solution for fast food restaurants. The second problem is more difficult to solve, due to the need for a cashier to collect money, as well as due to the fact that the restaurant should not be left without any employees. Here is where speech interaction for payment and ordering comes in. The customer can place an order, pay, and get information about the waiting time without leaving their seat.

This will save the customers and employees time, as well as reduce errors and misunderstandings during communication between a customer and a cashier.

The fast food industry is one of the fastest-growing markets for automation solutions. Its most famous representatives are McDonald's and Kentucky Fried Chicken (KFC). Both companies have already implemented self-service kiosks in many of their restaurants.

Most recently, the COVID-19 epidemic has accelerated the process of adopting new technologies. Using a voice-enabled drive-through service allows businesses to reduce the spread of infection and protect their employees. See Figure 5-2.

Figure 5-2. *COVID-19 prevention measures at a fast food restaurant*

Business Impact

The future of the fast food industry depends on the ability of restaurants to provide a better customer experience by automating repetitive and time-consuming tasks. The main problem that ordinary touchscreen, self-service kiosks have is that customers do not know how to use them, so there are many errors when entering orders. An error occurs once in every ten customer interactions. This leads to long queues in front of the kiosk. This is why voice interaction could be a solution. In natural conversation, a person does not consult the manual on how to pronounce words and people do not expect you to speak in an unnatural language (formal or slang). Therefore, using speech interaction seems like a natural solution for voice-controlled self-service stations.

There are many ways to use voice recognition and speech feedback in a restaurant. It can be used by customers as well as employees. The customer can use a kiosk to order food, pay for it, and get information about the waiting time. This is already common practice in some fast food restaurants, such as KFC.

The technology is not always advanced enough to understand the order accurately or to provide the right information at the right time. That is why there is a high rate of mistakes made by customers when placing orders. Speech recognition technology can reduce this problem significantly, because it can provide correct information, even when a customer spells something wrong or uses terminology not known to the machine. For example, if someone orders "a chicken nuggets with barbecue sauce," instead of giving an error message, the machine will recognize that this person wants chicken nuggets with barbecue sauce and give further instructions on how to proceed with the order. See Figure 5-3.

Figure 5-3. *People ordering at touchscreen kiosks*

Another possibility for using speech interaction in fast food restaurants is for employees who work at self-service kiosks or counters. Instead of typing all the information manually into the computer, they can just speak what they want to write into the computer system and then have the computer system convert their speech into text. This may also help restaurants reduce the rate of mistakes made by cashiers.

Speech recognition technology will also make it easier for retail businesses to provide information to their customers. For example, a self-service kiosk can give a customer information about dishes and drinks, as well as where they can find something. This can be achieved by using custom software with speech-recognition and speech-synthesis capabilities.

The third way to use speech-interaction technology is in terms of marketing and advertising. Some fast food restaurants are using virtual assistants like Amazon Alexa and Google Home to advertise their products on customers' smart speakers. This form of advertising may be especially useful for businesses that use shopping services such as Amazon Pantry or UberEats, because they can remind customers about their products whenever they see them in the list of deliveries.

Of course, there are some difficulties in using speech recognition technology in retail. For example, dealing with accents leads to the lowered accuracy. Speech-recognition systems work better with a "standard" accent and have a lower accuracy when processing an uncommon accent. This is why it is very important to have sufficient speech data from different speakers and different regions. See Figure 5-4.

Figure 5-4. *Different languages and accents still present a challenge for speech recognition systems*

Thus, the more data a speech recognition system has, the better its accuracy. A similar problem could occur between two different languages and dialects of one language (for example, between British English and American English). The second problem is that there should be a sufficient number of phrases for parsing in different situations (negative answers, questions, etc.). Additionally, there may be problems with background noise interfering with voice interaction.

This is especially relevant in fast food restaurants, when there is music playing or other sounds around the customers and employees. Finally, another problem may occur if people speak too quickly or too slow or they stutter. If this happens in the middle of an interaction with a customer, it would be difficult for the device to continue using its voice, as it would not know how to continue in a natural conversation with such a person due to lack of experience.

Related Knowledge

The main reason behind the significant increase in accuracy of automatic speech-recognition software and by extension its usability is deep learning. Similar to computer vision, before about 2010, speech recognition relied heavily on hand-crafted algorithms, which were complicated to program and rigid, and therefore they didn't perform well when encountering new accents or background sound. Anyone who used speech recognition to dial a phone number before 2010 knows what the quality of interaction was like. Deep learning has changed all that. In the two decades since, we've seen the accuracy of speech recognition improve from about 50% to nearly 95% with deep learning. See Figure 5-5.

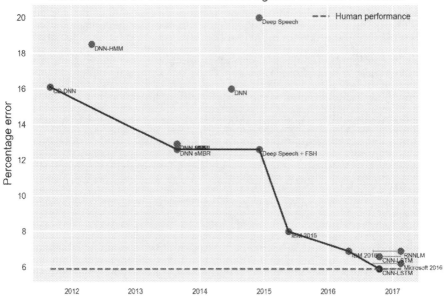

Figure 5-5. *Graph of decreasing word error rate over the last decade*

This is a revolution similar to the Internet and mobile computing revolutions. Deep learning has helped self-driving cars and many other domains dealing with large volumes of data. Speech is one such domain, whereby deep learning is making a huge difference in the way we interact with computers.

How Does Deep Learning Work with Speech Recognition?

Deep learning works for speech recognition on the assumption that any language or accent has a fixed set of distinguishing characteristics, and each word and sentence is made up of these characteristics to varying degrees. The problem with speech recognition is therefore reduced to finding these distinguishing characteristics in the speech signal and mapping them to words or characters. The recognition algorithm involves a sequence of steps:

1. **Collecting large amounts of data:** Collecting hundreds of hours of speech samples from multiple speakers of a language/accent to train the neural network on this data.

2. **Preprocessing the speech data:** This involves segmenting the speech into smaller frames of 100 ms-1000 ms and applying audio augmentations to the recordings.

3. **Transforming speech signals into a form that computers can understand:** Each of the small frames of the recorded speech is converted into a vector of parameters. These vectors are then stacked together and converted into a 15-dimensional vector. This vector is then passed through a neural network that learns the mapping between these parameters and words.

4. **Modeling:** A neural network is trained on the speech data and the mapping between these parameters and words.

5. **Making predictions:** Finally, the model is used to predict words given the parameters of the speech signal.

Deep learning for speech recognition provides the following benefits:

Very high accuracy: Speech recognition accuracy is measured in terms of "recognition rate," which is the percentage of words that are correctly recognized by the software. For English, this number is about 90%, which is similar to what a human can achieve.

Better quality of interaction: Deep learning for speech recognition has made possible natural language user interfaces for computers. For example, a user might say "Turn on the lights in the living room" and the computer would know to turn on the lights in the living room. This is just not possible with conventional speech recognition methods.

Speakers don't need to use a special microphone: Because deep learning can adapt to the speaker's accent, a speaker can use any microphone, which is a very big deal. The common way to collect speech data was to ask people to record themselves saying a few hundred sentences using a special microphone, which was expensive and cumbersome.

As you might have realized by now, training a speech-recognition model is not an easy endeavor. You need a large enough dataset and powerful training servers to achieve good accuracy. There is no need to reinvent the wheel with speech recognition, however. There are plenty of options available, both for online and offline speech recognition. Next, we look at some of them to give you an idea as to which approach is best suited for your specific scenario.

Online Speech-Recognition Service Providers

This section discusses the common online speech-recognition service providers on the market today.

- **Microsoft Azure:** With Azure (see Figure 5-6), you can have your own custom speech-recognition service up and running in under an hour. The flexibility of the platform allows developers to fine-tune the speech-recognition model.

Figure 5-6. *Microsoft Azure logo*

- **Amazon Alexa:** Alexa (see Figure 5-7) offers a number of features, including voice recognition, text-to-speech, and natural language processing. The service is available for mobile, web, and devices running Alexa, such as the Amazon Echo.

Figure 5-7. *Amazon Alexa logo*

- **Amazon Lex:** Lex i(see Figure 5-8) is a service for building conversational interfaces for applications using voice and text. The service helps to build applications with chat bots so users can interact naturally with your software using voice and text.

Figure 5-8. *Amazon Lex logo*

- **IBM Watson:** Watson (see Figure 5-9) is a cognitive computing platform that uses natural language processing and machine learning to reveal insights from large amounts of unstructured data.

Figure 5-9. *IBM Watson logo*

- **Google Cloud Speech API:** The Google Cloud Speech API (see Figure 5-10) is a REST API that enables you to convert audio to text. It supports over 80 languages, and it provides high-quality transcription and low latency.

Figure 5-10. *Google Cloud Speech API logo*

All of these online services charge for a certain amount of hours of audio/spoken utterances. While it is cheap to get started, if you have many devices running, the cost may become high enough for you to contemplate hybrid or offline solutions.

Offline speech recognition implies that the sound data is processed on the device, which has added benefits of lower latency and better privacy protection. The overall accuracy of offline speech recognition is not as high as of its online alternatives. This is because it has to run on the device, which has much less compute capacity than a server. However, if, as with the project in this chapter, the vocabulary for the task is limited to a certain area (such as ordering fast food using a drive-through), you can still achieve good results.

Offline Speech Recognition Frameworks

This section discusses the common offline speech-recognition service providers on the market today.

- **Mozilla DeepSpeech:** DeepSpeech (see Figure 5-11) is an open source, deep learning-based speech-recognition engine. It is capable of producing high-quality results in a wide variety of environments and languages. In 2020, because of internal reorganization in Mozilla, part of original DeepSpeech developers forked DeepSpeech into another project, called Coqui STT (pronounced "ko-kee"). The model inference engine and training scripts are open source and thus it is possible to use pretrained models or train your own.

Figure 5-11. *Mozilla DeepSpeech logo*

- ***Kaldi:*** This is an open source speech-recognition toolkit written in C++ for speech recognition and signal processing, freely available under the Apache License v2.0. Kaldi (see Figure 5-12) aims to provide software that is flexible and extensible, and is intended for use by ASR researchers for building a recognition system. While Kaldi is a powerful tool, it was recently sidelined by other projects, since it is difficult to set up for production and more suitable for research and experimentation.

Figure 5-12. *Kaldi logo*

- **Picovoice:** This an end-to-end platform for building voice products (see Figure 5-13.) Unlike Alexa and Google services, Picovoice runs entirely on-device while being comparatively accurate for a specific task. The main difference with Picovoice from other speech-recognition products is that it combines speech recognition with *intent* recognition. Using Picovoice, one can infer the user's intent from a naturally spoken utterance such as:

Figure 5-13. *Picovoice logo*

- "Hey Edison, set the lights in the living room to blue"

- Picovoice detects the occurrence of the custom wake word (Hey Edison), and then extracts the intent from the follow-on spoken command. Picovoice is free to use for prototyping, but enterprise customers need to purchase a license to use it.

- ***Fluent.ai:*** A set of solutions similar to Picovoice, enabling comparatively accurate and intuitive speech understanding solutions in a small footprint and low latency package. It's capable of running fully offline on small devices. See Figure 5-14.

Figure 5-14. *Fluent.ai logo*

For the demonstration project in this chapter, we're going to use Picovoice, since it focuses on speech-to-intent use cases with a specific domain, in this case ordering fast food.

Implementation

The Picovoice system consists of two main components: the wake-up word listener and the speech-to-intent recognition engine. The first one is extremely lightweight and consumes hardly any system resources, so it can be running 24/7 in background. Upon detection of the wake-up word, the speech-to-intent engine starts listening. When the user finishes the utterance, it outputs the intent in parsed form, for example:

```
{
  "intent": "changeColor",
  "slots": {
    "location": "living room",
    "color": "blue"
  }
}
```

This can be used to serve food to the customers according to their request. Additionally, you will see how to implement a simple on-device text-to-speech interface for confirming the order and conveying payment information to the customer. This will enable the entire process of ordering to be done hands-free and without using a screen.

1) Install Picovoice on Raspberry Pi 4 and try the pretrained Picovoice model for lights control.

2) Train a new speech-to-intent model for ordering fast food.

3) Combine the new speech-to-intent model with the text-to-speech engine.

Use the Pretrained Picovoice Model for Lights Control

First you need to install a microphone on the Raspberry Pi 4. The exact choice will be determined by your environmental conditions. For demonstration purposes, you can use a regular USB microphone if you have one lying around.

In this book, we use an affordable dual-microphone expansion board for Raspberry Pi, Seeed Studio's reSpeaker 2-mic Pi Hat (see Figure 5-15). It was developed based on WM8960, a low-power stereo codec. While only costing 9.90 dollars, the board is equipped with two microphones on both sides of the board for collecting sounds. It also provides three APA102 RGB LEDs, one user button, and two on-board grove interfaces for expanding your applications. What is more, a 3.5mm audio jack or a JST 2.0 speaker out are both available for audio output.

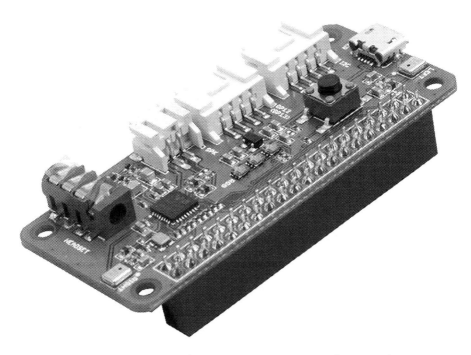

Figure 5-15. *Seeed Studio's reSpeaker 2-mic Hat for Raspberry Pi*

The first step is to install the drivers for your microphone. We use the Raspberry Pi OS 64-bit image as the starting point. For the purposes of this project, you can continue using the image you installed in Chapter 2. For some microphones, the drivers are already included with the Raspberry PI OS Linux kernel. If you opt for reSpeaker 2-mic Pi Hat, after installing the board on the Raspberry Pi 4 GPIO header, you'll need to install the drivers by executing a few simple commands:

```
sudo apt-get update
git clone https://github.com/respeaker/seeed-voicecard.git
cd seeed-voicecard
sudo ./install_arm64.sh
sudo reboot now
```

If you use a 32-bit image of the Raspberry Pi OS, you need to use the install.sh script instead of install_arm64.sh.

After the installation is finished, you can check for the presence of recording and playback devices with the aplay and arecord tools, as shown in Figure 5-16.

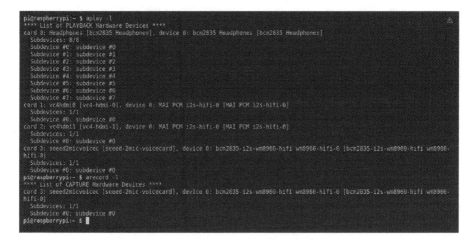

Figure 5-16. aplay -l and arecord -l execution results

Provided that the output of these commands on your system matches the output shown in Figure 5-16, your system is ready to start recording sound for inference.

For the next step, clone the Picovoice GitHub repository. Execute the following command from the Chapter_5 folder:

```
git clone https://github.com/Picovoice/picovoice.git exercise_1
cd exercise_1
git submodule update --init
pip3 install -r demo/python/requirements.txt
```

Then run the following command from the Picovoice folder to start the demo:

```
python3 demo/python/picovoice_demo_mic.py --keyword_path
resources/porcupine/resources/keyword_files/raspberry-pi/
picovoice_raspberry-pi.ppn --context_path resources/rhino/
resources/contexts/raspberry-pi/smart_lighting_raspberry-pi.rhn
```

Say the wake-up word ("picovoice") immediately followed by a command (e.g., "turn on the lights in the bedroom") to see intent being recognized and displayed in the terminal. See Figure 5-17.

Figure 5-17. *The result of the "Turn on the lights in the kitchen" voice command being recognized*

The next step is to train the custom model for fast food ordering using Picovoice Console.

Train a New Speech-to-Intent Model for Ordering Fast Food

To create a new speech-to-intent model for your application with Picovoice, go to `https://console.picovoice.ai/` and register an account there. Then access the console and choose the Rhino engine. Choose an empty template and click Create Context. For the purposes of this project, we use the name "fastfood," as shown in Figure 5-18.

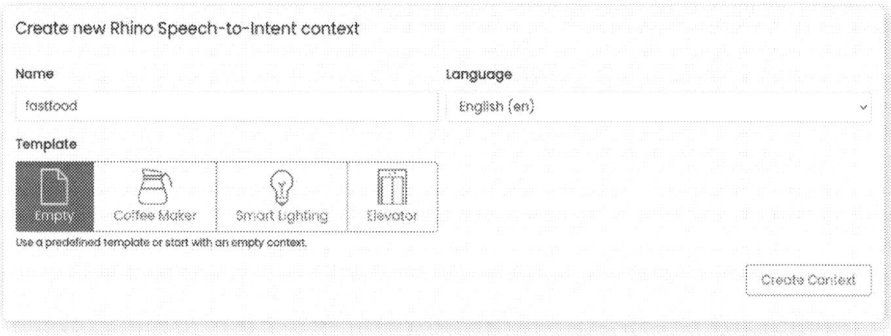

Figure 5-18. *Context creation interface*

In the newly opened window, create the necessary intents using the New Intent box in the left column. For this example, we are going to have three intents: orderFood, confirm, and cancel. See Figure 5-19.

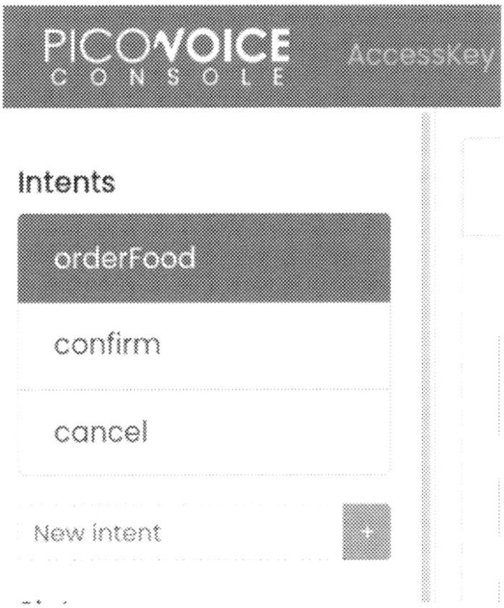

Figure 5-19. *Intents for the fast food context*

Add the slots next. When ordering food, the slots will be main, side, and drink. Add some food items to each of the slots as well. Here is what we used for this project (see Figure 5-20):

- Main: Hamburger, chicken burger, fish burger, wrap

- Side: French fries, salad, corn, onion rings

- Drink: Coke, orange juice, Sprite, Diet Coke

113

Figure 5-20. *Sample words for the main slot*

After that, go to the orderFood intent and add some sentences. Make them as descriptive as you can. See Figure 5-21.

Figure 5-21. *Sample sentences for the orderFood intent*

Different grammar/politeness variations of the same sentence can be created by placing options within square brackets. For syntax details, see the Rhino syntax cheat sheet at https://picovoice.ai/docs/tips/syntax-cheat-sheet/.

After you finish adding expressions, use the microphone button on the right column to test your context in-browser. Wait for the "Listening for voice input..." prompt. Speak the phrase that matches your expression. The results of the speech-to-intent inference appear in a box below the microphone button. See Figure 5-22.

Figure 5-22. *Inference results for "I would like a fish burger and french fries" sentence*

If it matches an expression, it will show the intent to which that expression belongs. If the spoken phrase did not match any expressions, it will report that it did not understand. To make the model more flexible, try exploring possible variations in different accents/phrasing by asking different people to test the model.

Once you're satisfied with the results, click the Save button and then train the model. Go to the Models tab and click Download, then choose Raspberry Pi as the target platform. After that, you can download the ZIP archive with a model file and copy it to your Raspberry Pi. If you use the Visual Studio Code IDE, that would be as simple as dragging and dropping the ZIP file to Chapter_5/exercise_2. Extract the ZIP archive with the following command from the exercise_2 folder:

```
unzip fastfood_raspberry-pi_v1.6.0.zip
```

Note   The name of the ZIP archive might differ.

After that, execute the following command from the Chapter_5 folder (NOT from the Chapter_5/exercise_2 folder!):

```
python3 demo/python/picovoice_demo_mic.py --keyword_path
resources/porcupine/resources/keyword_files/raspberry-pi/
picovoice_raspberry-pi.ppn --context_path fast-food.rhn
```

Make sure to change the context path argument to the exact path of the context file model you trained and copied to Raspberry Pi (if necessary, from your working directory). See Figure 5-23.

Figure 5-23. *Execution result on Raspberry Pi 4 with the reSpeaker hat*

Combine the New Speech-to-Intent Model with the Text-To-Speech Engine

The final step is to combine the custom speech-to-intent model with a simple text-to-speech engine in one Python script, so after understanding the order, the system will repeat it back to the customer and ask for confirmation. If the order is correct, the customer confirms it verbally or cancels it. Upon confirmation of the order, the total price and request for payment will be spoken.

You can find the finalized script in the chapter_5/exercise_3 folder of the book materials. Let's go through the most important parts of the script.

```
parser = argparse.ArgumentParser()
parser.add_argument('--context_path', help="Absolute path to
context file.")
args = parser.parse_args()

processor = OrderProcessor(args)
processor.main()
```

After doing the necessary imports on the top of the script, the script main try point is executed, which reads the argument with the context file location and then instantiates the OrderProcessor class with arguments from the command line. After that, the main() method of the AudioProcessor class is called.

117

The __init__ method of the OrderProcessor class contains an initialization of the "Porcupine" wake-up word engine with the default key word file set to "picovoice." The Rhino speech-to-intent engine has a context file specified in the arguments to the script. Another important step is preparing the audio stream with start_audio_stream_method() and instantiating the text-to-speech engine for the talk back function.

```python
def __init__(self, args):
  self.wakeword_engine = pvporcupine.
  create(keywords=['picovoice'])
  self.wakeword_engine_frame_length = self.wakeword_engine.
  frame_length

  self.nlu_engine = pvrhino.create(library_path=pvrhino.
  LIBRARY_PATH,
  model_path=pvrhino.MODEL_PATH,
  context_path=args.context_path)
  self.nlu_engine_frame_length = self.nlu_engine.frame_length

  self.spinner = Halo(text='Listening', spinner='dots')

  self.start_audio_input()
  self.engine = pyttsx3.init()
  self.menu_prices = {"hamburger":1.99,
  "wrap":1.3,
  "chicken burger": 1.1,
  "fish burger": 1.5,
  "french fries": 0.5,
  "salad": 0.6,
  "corn": 0.4,
  "coke": 0.2,
  "sprite": 0.2,
  "diet coke": 0.2,
  "orange juice": 0.2}
```

Once these are all ready, the main logic of the program is executed in the main() method. The important parts of the order food flow are separated into methods of the OrderProcessor class. First you wait for the keyword, then a TTS greeting is played, then you use the Rhino speech-to-intent engine to parse the customer's order. Next, the order is parsed. The system repeats the order back to the customer using TTS and waits for confirmation or cancellation.

After the order is confirmed, the cost is output and the customer is asked to pay using a QR code. The actual QR code payment code is not included in this example, but you can use the Paypal payment processing example in Chapter 3 to add this feature.

```python
def main(self):
  while True:
    try:
      self.wait_for_keyword()
      self.speak('Welcome to order at Robo Fast Food.')
      time.sleep(0.5)
      self.order, phrase = self.process_order()
      self.speak(phrase)
      time.sleep(0.5)
      result = self.wait_for_confirmation()
      if result:
        total = sum([self.menu_prices[item] for item in
        self.order])
        phrase = "Your order total is {} USD. Please scan the
        QR code to pay. Enjoy your meal!".format(total)
      else:
        phrase = "Alright. Welcome to come back again!"
      self.speak(phrase)
```

See the example code for detailed content of other `OrderProcessor` methods.

Before you run the `exercise_3` code, you need to install some additional dependencies. You can do that with the following (from the `exercise_3` folder):

```
sudo apt-get install portaudio19-dev espeak
pip3 install -r requirements.txt
```

You can also run the example with the following command, from the `exercise_3` folder:

```
python3 porcupine_demo_mic.py --context_path [path-to-your-rhino-model]
```

Pro Tips

There are multiple improvements that can be made to the example script and setup you created in this project. If you want your device to handle more queries, you can use a generic speech-to-text engine, for example DeepSpeech or one of the described cloud-based solutions, which have extremely high accuracy, even in noisy environments. Then you would create a text-to-intent model based on your use case. These are normally easier to train, since the dataset for the training is text and not raw audio. Such a setup would be more flexible and allow for more natural customer interaction.

While we used regular Raspberry Pi 4 in this chapter, it is definitely possible to deploy the project on a Raspberry Pi 4 Compute Module installed on a custom-made carrier board similar to the one described in Chapter 3 or using reTerminal with a microphone array attached. See Figure 5-24.

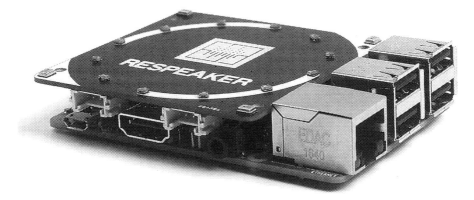

Figure 5-24. *Raspberry Pi 3B+ with reSpeaker 4-mic*

Some other possible expansions include a touchscreen for adding visual feedback to interaction, a camera for face recognition payment processing, and a QR code scanner for other payment options.

Since it is not the main focus of this chapter, for the text-to-speech engine, we used the most basic engine available to be deployed on Raspberry Pi 4—espeak. Although it is easy to set up and use, it sounds a bit robotic and there are better options available, both online and offline.

Summary

This chapter explained the main principles of speech recognition and then demonstrated a working principle of using this technology, with an example of a speech recognition-enabled, fast food drive-through service kiosk. The kiosk can take customers' orders in natural language using the Picovoice Rhino speech-to-intent engine and communicate with those customers with the help of the espeak text-to-speech engine.

CHAPTER 6

Employee Attendance Management System

Problem Overview

Biometric technology is already a big part of our lives and many people don't realize just how common biometric technology is. In part, the term "biometric" itself seems too technical, and that makes it hard for people to understand what it is.

The easiest way to understand how biometrics is the future of security is to ask yourself if you'd prefer to memorize multiple PIN codes and "strong" passwords or just present a fingerprint. More and more, we'll adopt fingerprints. Biometrics helps get rid of keys, cards, or tokens, so there is no need to carry around a bunch of things just to prove that you are who you say you are. Biometrics only requires your physical being, making security more convenient. See Figure 6-1.

© Elaine Wu, Dmitry Maslov 2022
E. Wu and D. Maslov, *Raspberry Pi Retail Applications*,
https://doi.org/10.1007/978-1-4842-7951-9_6

Figure 6-1. *Commercial fingerprint scanners use a form of biometric identification*

And of course, biometrics removes the potential for fraud. PIN codes, keys, and tokens can be stolen, forged, hacked, and shared between users—something that biometrics can help prevent with unique characteristics. But probably the most important thing about biometrics is that the technology is constantly evolving. So it's not just about using a fingerprint or facial recognition to gain access to a building or to your phone. The technology is fast improving new forms like vein recognition and heartbeat detection are also included into biometrics.

Fingerprint recognition is widely used to control access to government buildings, board rooms, computer facilities, museums, banks, airports, offices, hotels, etc. Face recognition is increasingly used for security purposes. Face recognition can be used as an identification such as a passport, as well as for access control. Iris recognition is widely used in the fields of immigration, border control, security, and identification. Voice recognition is rapidly improving and is used for human machine interaction and as a method of authentication.

Biometric authentication is one of the most popular authentication technologies. It has a number of advantages compared to other authentication technologies, such as:

- High security and assurance

- User experience is convenient and fast

- Non-transferable

- Near spoof-proof

Biometric authentication includes fingerprint authentication, face recognition, voice recognition (not to be confused with speech recognition), and iris recognition. See Figure 6-2.

Figure 6-2. *Iris recognition is among the most secure forms of biometric authentication and is rarely used in commercial settings*

The most widely used biometric authentication is fingerprint authentication, which matches an individual's unique fingerprint patterns. New fingerprint scanners can even detect vascular patterns in people's fingers. Using a supported fingerprint scanner and Python library, it is relatively straightforward to recognize fingerprints on a Linux-based embedded computer (Raspberry Pi). In the retail industry, fingerprint sensors can be used for time tracking and punch-in/punch-out processes. Additionally, HR departments can benefit from further analysis of this data. By the end of this chapter, we will have built a system for identifying attendance and collecting data that can be used to manage human resources. In retail check-in machines, fingerprint authentication machines can also be used. To verify our identities, we will scan and store fingerprints on the Raspberry Pi.

Business Impact

For small- and medium-sized retail business, the most important uses of commercially available biometric technologies are as follows:

- **Building access.** Originally reserved for government and corporate offices, the convenience and affordability of the technology have made fingerprint scanners accessible to anyone who needs to protect their private space. Businesses can now use biometric access control for a range of security benefits. Biometric systems are great way for businesses to preserve employees' productivity since it reduces the amount of time spent entering and exiting a building. Often, time wasted waiting to gain access to a building can mean significant losses, sometimes amounting up to 3 percent of productivity. The other aspect is security, where biometrics plays a key role. Fingerprint scanners or facial recognition cameras will deny access to anyone not registered, which provides a level of protection that passwords can't offer. This is particularly appropriate in a secure area containing large amounts of valuable material or machinery.

- **Attendance/time-tracking.** At many companies, employees clock in by entering a four-digit code printed on their ID badges (see Figure 6-3). This is often a problem for assistant department heads and staff, since they usually have multiple departments to attend. In addition, these codes are printed on the badges, meaning that once people have left the department, they are no longer visible to security. Biometrics can resolve this problem. This technology can clock in every employee on company premises without requiring their ID badge or any other secondary form of verification.

Figure 6-3. *Employee attendance is often recorded by using employee ID badges or identity cards*

Although this technology offers financial savings to your organization, there are various social benefits too. An employer benefits from a system that keeps their employees safe. With the absence of a fixed clock in time, you can measure working hours accurately and settle any complaint regarding hours worked. Biometric systems are used to clock into the building, but their use often extends to timekeeping. There are numerous benefits to integrating biometrics into your company's system. The system can only match the biometrics of the authorized employees registered in the system, so time theft is prevented. This leaves minimal room for error since the employees have no control over the system.

Time and attendance is combined with a self-service portal called *my time.* At its simplest, a time and attendance system records the log-in and log-out times of employees based on their fingerprints or facial scans. From that information, it calculates how much time is spent at the office and how much time is spent away, including lunch breaks. By linking this to the rest of the company's information systems, managers can produce reports when needed.

These two applications alone can have a profound effect on business efficiency, especially for the small and medium business that have a limited number of staff members. For these businesses, biometrics can simply replace logbooks since they are automated systems that do not require manual work. Moreover, the efficiency of the employees will increase due to the less time they spent on entry exit.

For larger businesses, the cost-effectiveness still exists, since you only have to pay once for the installation instead of paying someone to clock in for you. In a large business environment, these systems can be integrated to form a single entity and solve several problems. This in turn eliminates redundant manpower and simplifies the management of businesses, especially by allowing real-time employee monitoring, thus reducing risks and maximizing benefits.

Related Knowledge

Everyone in the world has a unique fingerprint. A fingerprint scanner is a tool that can scan fingerprints and convert them into binary codes. The converted fingerprint is then stored in the device. Fingerprint scanning can be done optically with a camera using the visible light frequency spectrum. Modern commercial fingerprint scanners have two major circuits—the true pick-up sensor, which is responsible for capturing the fingerprint images, and the preprocessing circuit, which is responsible for processing the images captured. Besides the necessary chip mounted on the fingerprint scanner, a PC system needs an operating system to recognize the fingerprint scanner, or to send standard commands that may be needed to search among images of fingerprints stored on the scanner if the device has the right software.

To operate the system, you place your finger on the flat area of the scanner, usually colored black or gray ,with an imaging sensor made up of one or more rows of photo diodes. Normally it takes just a few seconds for the scanner to scan the image of the fingerprint. The scanner's imaging sensor analyzes the fingerprint within the field of view of the image scanner. See Figure 6-4.

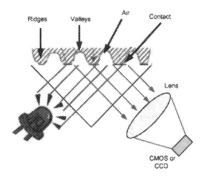

Figure 6-4. *Working principle of typical optical fingerprint sensor*

The image scanner starts capturing an image when it is in contact with the finger, and the preprocessing circuit turns the signals into voltage. This voltage will appear in the PC when it has received enough information to digitally render the fingerprint in grayscale. This can be done with an analog or digital circuit. The fingerprint intelligence is sent to the computer, where the computer identifies the fingerprint and compares the scan to an existing scan on record. More advanced scanners reduce the preprocessing time by automating the process and converting the captured fingerprint to a numeric fingerprint image. This numeric image is stored in EEPROM and is automatically compared with stored fingerprint profiles; it cannot be retroactively accessed by bad actors.

For this project, as you are designing an automatic attendance-tracking system, you will also use a motion sensor to trigger a fingerprint-scanning process when a person is detected in the vicinity of the device. Additionally, a simple LED is connected to the system to give feedback to the user on the current state of the system.

Here is a full list of the hardware used for this project:

- Raspberry Pi 4

- AS608 Fingerprint Sensor

- Grove PIR Motion Sensor

- Grove LED

- USB-to-serial converter

- Grove Base Hat for Raspberry Pi

The Fingerprint Sensor

The AS608 Fingerprint Sensor (see Figure 6-5) is an optical fingerprint sensor module that makes fingerprint detection and verification simple. We chose to use the fingerprint sensor, powered by the AS608 chip, to obtain a fingerprint image, feature calculation, and feature matching. AS608 is an integrated optical fingerprint chip with a fingerprint algorithm inside. The AS608 module uses an 8-pin control interface. The power supply voltage supports 3.3V. There are two communication buses: serial communication (TX, RX) and USB communication. The AS608 manual includes a related serial port instruction set, so you can use these instructions to call the fingerprint algorithm to achieve the functions you need for the application. You can enroll up to 100 new fingerprints and store them in the on-board Flash memory. A built-in LED in AS608 is used to convey the information about the working state of the sensor.

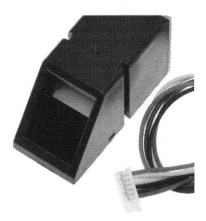

Figure 6-5. *AS608 optical fingerprint sensor*

Not only can you use this fingerprint sensor with Arduino or Raspberry Pi boards following with Adafruit libraries, but it's also easy to integrate the AS608 module into other microcontrollers, such as STM32 boards through TTL serial.

The PIR Motion Sensor

PIR refers to a passive infrared sensor and it measures infrared light radiating from objects in its field of view. PIR motion sensors are most often used in PIR-based motion detectors, such as security alarms and automatic lighting applications. Figure 6-6 shows the Grove PIR motion sensor.

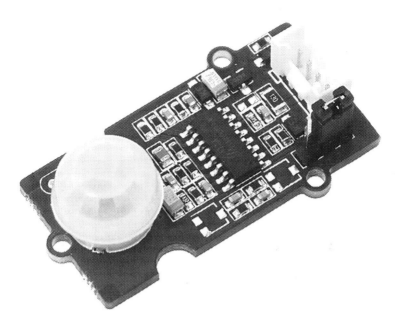

Figure 6-6. *Grove PIR motion sensor, source: Seeed*

Generally, PIR can detect animal/human movement in a requirement range, which is determined by the specs of the specific sensor. The detector does not emit any energy but passively receives it, detecting infrared radiation from the environment.

Here is the range of different PIR sensors:

- Indoor passive infrared: Detection distances range from 25cm to 20m.

- Indoor curtain-type: Detection distances range from 25cm to 20m.

- Outdoor passive infrared: Detection distances range from 10 meters to 150 meters.

- Outdoor passive infrared curtain detector: Detection distances range from 10 meters to 150 meters.

The Software for Interfacing with the Sensor and Storing the Data

Adafruit has written both Arduino library and Python library to help you run the fingerprint detection program in ten minutes. The library supports both enrollment and search for fingerprints. Once you enroll fingerprints, an assigning ID number is assigned correspond to each print for you to search later. You need to look for the exact ID that has been photographed and verify if the ID is enrolled. See Figure 6-7.

Figure 6-7. *Fingerprint PNG picture that can be saved when enrolling the fingerprint*

Pandas (see Figure 6-8) is a fast, powerful, flexible, and easy-to-use open source data analysis library for Python. It is a BSD-licensed library that provides high-performance, easy-to-use data structures, and data-analysis tools for reading and writing data between in-memory data structures and different formats: CSV and text files, Microsoft Excel, and SQL databases.

Figure 6-8. *Pandas logo*

The source code is hosted on GitHub at https://github.com/pandas-dev/pandas.

Implementation

The implementation consists of the following steps:

1) Wire the modules.

2) Install the software and register the fingerprints.

3) Combine the motion sensor with the fingerprint sensor.

You can continue using the Raspberry Pi OS 64-bit image you installed in Chapter 2 as the starting point for this project.

Wire the Modules

There are different models of the AS608 sensor available on the market and it is important to wire the sensor properly. See Figure 6-9.

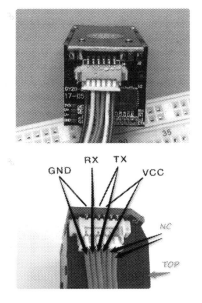

Figure 6-9. *Two different variants of AS608 fingerprint scanner module. Source: Adafruit*

If your sensor has different color wires, the first wire from the left should be the black ground wire. Then the two data pins—RX is the white wire and TX is the green wire. Then the red power wire. Alternatively, if your sensor has all the same color wires, the first wire from the left is the ground, then the two data pins, then the power.

You can use an external USB-to-serial converter or the built-in UART on the Pi's TX/RX pins. Figure 6-10 shows an example of wiring the USB-to-serial converter.

Figure 6-10. *Fingerprint sensor wiring to USB-to-serial converter. Source: Adafruit*

- Sensor VCC (red wire) to USB 5V or 3V (red wire on USB console cable)

- Sensor GND (black wire) to USB Ground (black wire)

- Sensor RX (white wire) to USB TX (green wire)

- Sensor TX (green wire) to USB RX (white wire)

To use the Raspberry Pi built-in UART to wire, make sure you disable the serial console and enable the serial port hardware in `raspi-config`, if you choose a built-in UART. See Figure 6-11.

```
sudo raspi-config
```

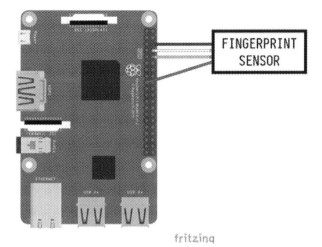

Figure 6-11. *Fingerprint scanner wiring to Raspberry Pi GPIO. Source: Adafruit*

Then connect the sensor to the Raspberry Pi GPIO header with jumper wires, using the following information as a reference.

- Pi ground wires sensor GND (black)

- Pi TX wires sensor RX (white)

- Pi RX wires sensor TX (green)

- Pi 3.3V wires sensor VCC (red)

You can look up the Raspberry Pi GPIO pins chart to wire the sensor. See Figure 6-12.

Raspberry Pi Pinout

	Pin	Pin	
3v3 Power	1	2	5v Power
GPIO 2 (I2C1 SDA)	3	4	5v Power
GPIO 3 (I2C1 SCL)	5	6	Ground
GPIO 4 (GPCLK0)	7	8	GPIO 14 (UART TX)
Ground	9	10	GPIO 15 (UART RX)
GPIO 17	11	12	GPIO 18 (PCM CLK)
GPIO 27	13	14	Ground
GPIO 22	15	16	GPIO 23
3v3 Power	17	18	GPIO 24
GPIO 10 (SPI0 MOSI)	19	20	Ground
GPIO 9 (SPI0 MISO)	21	22	GPIO 25
GPIO 11 (SPI0 SCLK)	23	24	GPIO 8 (SPI0 CE0)
Ground	25	26	GPIO 7 (SPI0 CE1)
GPIO 0 (EEPROM SDA)	27	28	GPIO 1 (EEPROM SCL)
GPIO 5	29	30	Ground
GPIO 6	31	32	GPIO 12 (PWM0)
GPIO 13 (PWM1)	33	34	Ground
GPIO 19 (PCM FS)	35	36	GPIO 16
GPIO 26	37	38	GPIO 20 (PCM DIN)
Ground	39	40	GPIO 21 (PCM DOUT)

Figure 6-12. Raspberry Pi 4 GPIO pinout guide, source: pinout.xyz

To connect the Grove PIR motion sensor and the Grove LED, use the GrovePi Base Hat. This will allow you to avoid using jumper cables and use the more convenient Grove wires instead. Connect the PIR motion sensor to the D18 socket and the Grove LED to the D24 socket. You are now finished setting up the wiring. See Figure 6-13.

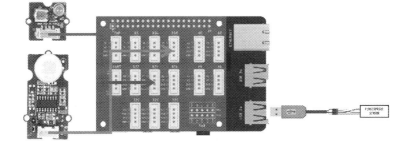

Figure 6-13. *Everything is wired up!*

Install the Software and Register the Fingerprints

Start the SSH connection from the bash terminal or (recommended) using Visual Studio Code as described in Chapter 2. Change the directory to Chapter_6/.

From your command line, run the following commands to install the Adafruit Fingerprint sensor library:

```
git clone https://github.com/adafruit/Adafruit_CircuitPython_
Fingerprint.git exercise_1
cd exercise_1
pip3 install -e .
```

It is possible to install the Adafruit CircuitPython Fingerprint library from Python Package Index (PyPi) with the following:

```
pip3 install adafruit-circuitpython-fingerprint
```

However, we chose to use a local install instead, because we need to use the example scripts for sensor testing and user enrollment.

To test the fingerprint sensor, run this command from the exercise_1 folder (see Figure 6-14):

python3 examples/fingerprint_simpletest_rpi.py

Figure 6-14. *The fingerprint sensor has been successfully recognized so the main menu is displayed*

Note   If you get an error saying "RuntimeError: Failed to read data from sensor", check your wiring and make sure the baud rate is set to 57600.

If you are directly connecting the sensor to Raspberry Pi 4 UART, comment out line 14 and uncomment line 17 in fingerprint_simpletest_rpi.py. See Figure 6-15.

Figure 6-15. *Changes necessary to use the Raspberry Pi UART instead of an external USB-to-serial converter*

Start the enrollment process by typing e and pressing Enter after starting `fingerprint_simpletest_rpi.py`. Enroll and store your fingerprint image as ID 1. You'll notice that the sensor starts flashing.

After clicking the fingerprint sensor, if the image has been successfully taken, you will see the output in Figure 6-16, which means the fingerprint image has been properly stored as a template model with an ID number.

Figure 6-16. *Successful enrollment results*

If the two prints don't match, or the device fails to store the image to generate a template, you will see the error message in Figure 6-17.

Figure 6-17. *Failure of fingerprint enrollment*

Repeat the procedure until it is successful. Make sure you press your finger tight against the sensor and the sensor surface is clean and unobstructed.

When your finger is successfully enrolled, enter f in the main menu of `fingerprint_simpletest_rpi.py`. You'll notice that the sensor starts flashing. Press the same finger you used for enrollment against the sensor and the program will print "Searching" while trying to match your fingerprint inside internal storage. See Figure 6-18.

Figure 6-18. *Fingerprint scanned and found in database*

If the recognition is successful, it will print the ID and confidence of the fingerprint match.

You can also remove the fingerprint model saved to the system by entering d in the main menu of `fingerprint_simpletest_rpi.py`.

For the LED and the motion sensor, you need to download and run a script that will install the `grove.py` Python 3 library on your Raspberry Pi:

```
curl -sL https://github.com/Seeed-Studio/grove.py/raw/master/
install.sh | sudo bash -s -
```

The Grove Base Hat for Raspberry Pi provides digital/analog/I2C/PWM/UART port (see Figure 6-19). With the help of a built-in MCU, a 12-bit 8-channel ADC is also available for Raspberry Pi. There are more than 60 Grove modules that support the Grove Base Hat for Raspberry Pi. There are more than 350 kinds of Grove modules created by the Seeed Grove plug-and-play ecosystem to help you quickly prototype in a no-wiring way. Seeed will also update more Grove compatibility in use with Raspberry Pi.

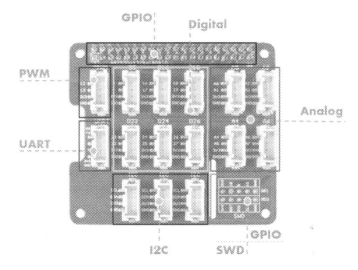

Figure 6-19. *Grove Base Hat for Raspberry Pi, source: Seeed*

After installing the grove.py library and connecting an LED and a motion sensor, you can now test your hardware.

To do that, change the directory to Chapter_6/exercise_2 and run the following command in the bash terminal:

```
python3 test_led_motion_sensor.py
```

When motion is detected, the program will start blinking an LED.

If you have successfully verified these steps and found that the hardware connected to your Raspberry Pi 4 works, you can start to use the example Python file to design your system architecture!

Combining the Motion Sensor with the Fingerprint Sensor

The sample application can be found in the Chapter_6/working_project folder. The program logic of the sample application consists of a few important parts.

First, you get the PIN numbers as arguments and create Blinker and Motion sensor objects. The UART object is created on the ttyUSB0 port (change that if you are connecting the fingerprint sensor directly to the Raspberry Pi, without a USB-to-serial converter). The AdafruitFingerprint class instance is initialized with a newly created UART object.

```
if __name__ == '__main__':

if len(sys.argv) < 3:
print('Usage: {} led_pin sensor_pin, e.g. python3 attendance.py
16 24'.format(sys.argv[0]))
sys.exit(1)

blinker = Blinker(int(sys.argv[1]))
motion_sensor = MotionSensor(int(sys.argv[2]))
uart = serial.Serial("/dev/ttyUSB0", baudrate=57600, timeout=1)
finger = adafruit_fingerprint.Adafruit_Fingerprint(uart)

main()
```

If there is a person approaching the fingerprint machine, the PIR motion sensor will detect the motion and the main application logic will start running.

```
def main():
while True:

while not motion_sensor.is_activated():
time.sleep(0.05)

print('Motion detected.')
```

The system will try to collect the fingerprint five times. If no fingerprint is detected, it will go back to waiting mode.

```
tries = 0
user_input = False
finger_found = True

while not get_fingerprint():
time.sleep(.05)
tries += 1
print("Num of tries: ", tries)
if tries >= 5:
print("No finger detected")
blinker.blink(0.1, 3)
finger_found = False
break
```

If a fingerprint is successfully detected, the program gets the system time and appends the ID of the recognized finger with the time stamp to the attendance.csv file.

```
if finger_found:
date = time.asctime(time.localtime(time.time()))
id = finger.finger_id

dict = {'id': [id], 'datetime': [date]}
print("Saving data: ", dict)
blinker.blink(1, 3)
df = pd.DataFrame(dict)
df.to_csv('attendance.csv', mode = 'a', header = False,
index=False)
```

The Grove LED - Red module is used to indicate the current status of the device. It is inactive when no motion is detected. If the system was activated but no fingerprint was found (an error state), the LED will blink very quickly (10Hz) for three seconds. If the fingerprint-matching function returned True(Success state), that means the device recognized the fingerprint and the fingerprint ID number. It saves the punch in/out date and to the csv. file, and the LED will blink slowly(1Hz) for three seconds. See Figure 6-20.

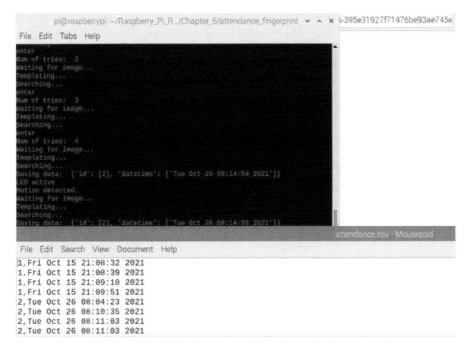

Figure 6-20. *Motion was detected and the fingerprint was successfully matched and saved to the .csv file*

In order to run a working example, execute the following steps:

1. Connect all the sensors and connect the power to the Raspberry Pi 4.

2. Start the application with the following:

```
python3 working_project/attendance.py 24 16
```

Run this command from the Chapter_6 folder and remember to change the PIN numbers if you connected the LED and/or motion sensor to other pins.

3. When there is a human approaching the device, the PIR motion sensor will pick up the motion and the fingerprint sensor's internal LED will start blinking.

4. Place your finger (already enrolled in the previous section with fingerprint_simpletest_rpi.py) on the fingerprint sensor.

5. If the finger matches one of the templates stored in the sensor, its ID and current date/time will be appended to the attendance.csv file. If the fingerprint does not match any of the templates stored in the sensor, the system will go into waiting mode. See Figure 6-21.

1	Fri Oct 15 21:08:32 2021
1	Fri Oct 15 21:08:39 2021
1	Fri Oct 15 21:09:10 2021
1	Fri Oct 15 21:09:51 2021

Figure 6-21. *Database stored as a .csv file; ID is the first column and date/time is the second*

Pro Tips

Using a SQL Database

Instead of using a `.csv` file, you could save the data in SQL databases and upload them to the cloud. Fingerprint datasets are a kind of repeating or structured data, and you may need to process a large number of fingerprints due to daily traffic. Using spreadsheet applications such as .csv files, Excel, or Numbers may lead to the following problems:

- You can only undo or start over with accidental errors.

- It is impossible to replicate all function steps in Excel, such as VLOOKUP.

- It is slow to run a large number of datasets in Excel (my laptop gets stuck very often).

- It is hard to share big Excel files via email (unless you use a Google online spreadsheet).

Excel is easy to use, with functions of merging cells, creating tables and charts, and processing hundreds of different functions. However, Excel also brings more waiting time for complex work.

What Is SQL?

SQL (Structured Query Language) is a language used for programming and interacting with databases, while Excel is a program that you can run in Linux, macOS, and Windows. By using SQL, your data will be stored in a relational database composed of tables, with rows and columns. You can search the database by sending queries to the database in SQL. The database receives these queries and makes your request or change, such as creating tables and modifying data in different rows and columns.

SQL vs. Excel

SQL is much faster than Excel. It can take several minutes in SQL to search and match a large amount of data, whereas it might take an hour to process in Excel. Excel can technically process a million rows, but you have to run multiple functions. Compared with the pain points of Excel's non-copyable steps of functions and analysis, using SQL is more collaborative and traceable.

What Is SQL in the Cloud?

Data comes in different formats, and there is no storage solution is suitable for all kinds of data. In this example, we need to consider using structured data. Structured data, sometimes called relational data, is data that follows a strict model and has the same fields or attributes. The shared mode allows easy searching of such data using query languages such as SQL. This feature makes this type of data ideal for applications such as CRM systems, reservations, and inventory management. Structured data is usually stored in database tables with rows and columns and key columns to indicate the relationship between one row in the table and the data in another row in another table. For example, fingerprint ID and date/time match.

Structured data is simple because it is easy to enter, query, and analyze. All the data follows the same format. However, forcing a consistent structure also means that the evolution of the data is more difficult because each record must be updated to conform to the new structure. You can save the database locally, however, suppose you need to share this CRM with all employees in different locations around the world. You need to build a cloud-based SQL database, whereby you can query any data in the cloud.

You can also use Azure SQL Database, which is built on the Microsoft Azure cloud operating system and runs on cloud computing's Database as a Service. It is an implementation of cloud storage and provides network-based application data. Azure SQL Database is a platform-as-a-service (PaaS) that can automatically handle a lot of management functions, such as upgrades, patching, backups, and monitoring, without user involvement.

A Dedicated Raspberry Pi 4 Hat with a Fingerprint Sensor

Apart from using a standalone sensor, there are accessories to simplify fingerprint scanning and matching with Raspberry Pi. Figure 6-22 shows an example of such an expansion board (also called a "hat").

Figure 6-22. *CNX SOFTWARE: PiFinger connected to a laptop or Raspberry Pi over USB, or over the 40-pin header. Access control demo.*

The SB Components team crowdfunded the world's first fingerprint Hat through Kickstarter in 2020 (see Figure 6-23). This Hat offers a fingerprint sensor, built with a Cortex-M23 TrustZone and a high-speed UART interface as well as an on-chip crypto-accelerator from the Nuvoton MCU. There is also an on-board 2D Capacitive, which can scan an 8mmx8mm square with a resolution of 176px x 176px. There is also an OLED display and several LEDs used for indicators. The Hat uses a 2D capacitive fingerprint scanner. As the Hat supports serial/UART communication, you can also use Python to program it.

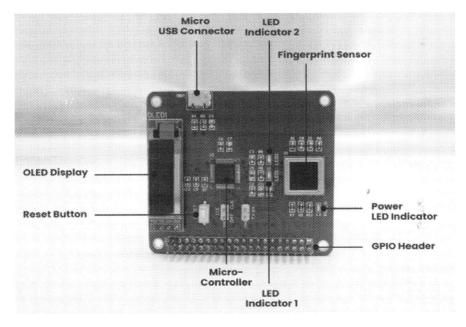

Figure 6-23. *PiFinger by SB Components, Ltd*

Summary

This chapter talked about how to quickly build a prototype of a fingerprint attendance-taking device, collect fingerprint data, and use a Python data analysis toolkit to create a dataset using the data stored in the program. In order to use the sensor, you need to download the Adafruit libraries and change some code to use other sensors like a PIR motion sensor and LED. With the help of the libraries and plug-and-play access using Grove sensors, it's easier and faster to verify the functions. You learned how to wire the sensor by identifying GPIOs on the Raspberry Pi and how to set up a programming environment by installing Python libraries. Furthermore, if you have a large amount of data, you need to consider using cloud tools.

CHAPTER 7

Advertisement Display

Problem Overview

Advertisement is a crucial element of any business's success. It's hard to say when people started advertising their goods, but it certainly happened long ago. Advertising has been carried out in newspapers and on TV, yet a large chunk of advertisement activities have moved online to the Internet. Physical outdoor and indoor advertisements still hold a significant importance, both for large and small companies. For retail companies, offline physical advertisement—such as posters, banners, leaflets, and so on—provide a cheap and convenient way to reach the local pool of potential customers. However, posters and banners have a significant disadvantage—they're static. Once the picture is printed and advertisement is placed in the location, changing anything—no matter how small—will require an amount of labor equaling or exceeding the amount used for initial installation. See Figure 7-1.

© Elaine Wu, Dmitry Maslov 2022
E. Wu and D. Maslov, *Raspberry Pi Retail Applications*,
https://doi.org/10.1007/978-1-4842-7951-9_7

Figure 7-1. *A sensor-enabled advertisement screen displaying a context-relevant ad*

That problem can be solved by using a digital medium for displaying advertisements. An LCD or OLED screen connected to a microcontroller or a single-board computer can display static graphics and video footage, which can be changed depending on time of the day, the location, and other factors, such as the weather. By adding sensors to the system, you can even make your installation interactive!

Business Impact

The whole point of signage is to connect to customers and grab their attention. Unlike paper signs, which only use pictures and text, digital signs can display every kind of media, from promotional videos to advanced moving graphics. It is widely known in marketing circles that customers have a far more positive response to these kinds of materials than they do to stationary images or blocks of text. Even something as simple as a colorful sale sign can be far more effective if it is flashing or spinning around on a screen. By using creative design when planning the content of your digital sign displays, you can engage fully with customers and ultimately boost your sales. See Figure 7-2.

Figure 7-2. *A row of advertisement screens at the exhibition*

Using their cloud networks, businesses can change what is being displayed on their digital signs instantaneously, which makes them the most versatile mediums for promotion and sales. One way that many businesses are using digital signs is to run no-notice sales when they have a surplus of a particular item or when that item is about to be taken off the shelves.

Digital signage streamlines every step of this process, making it cheaper, easier, and quicker to launch a new season across multiple stores. By using a cloud-based digital signage system, businesses can design their promotional materials themselves and instantaneously upload the new season's signs to every screen across their locations. Not only does this save money on printing, transportation, and employees, it also helps to save paper and fuel. Many businesses are judged on their green policies, so this is an ideal way to appeal to environmentally conscious customers.

Digital signage has been used to help people navigate airports, helping customers find everything from restrooms to their gate. The ever-growing travel industry has been a target for digital signage, as airports and cruise ships strive to attract customers with a variety of services and amenities. Digital signage has been used to keep customers informed about their flights, as well as to find other information, such as maps and directions to parking lots and other local businesses, and help customers navigate the airport once they have landed.

Other advantages of using LCD screens as billboards are that they are easy to set up, can be easily moved around, and come in a variety of sizes. The digital signage market offers numerous benefits for businesses. Because digital signage is so versatile, it can be used to offer just about any kind of service or product. No matter what the business is, whether it is a fast food restaurant, a bank, or a car dealership, there is a way for digital signs to help them reach their audience.

Digital signage is also an effective way for businesses to get their message across to the public quickly. The time it takes to get your message across to your audience is key in the success of the campaign. Digital signage allows businesses to reach their audience faster, which in turn increases their ability to make sales. Digital signage can also be used to do research on customers. This is because digital signage allows businesses to incorporate things like surveys into their advertisements, which can then be used to get information about the audience. This type of information can then be used when creating future advertisements, so that businesses are able to better target the audience that will buy their products or use their services. Digital signage also allows for businesses to have creative freedom when it comes to the ads they create. Digital signage is an effective way for businesses to monitor their advertisements because it allows them to track the number of people who view their advertisements or who take the surveys that are used in advertisements. This kind of information is crucial for businesses, because it allows them to determine if their ad campaign was successful.

Related Knowledge

Raspberry Pi 4 is a great choice for creating a digital advertising screen, since it has 2 mini-HDMI ports capable of outputting 4k resolution video at 60 FPS. Its rich networking capabilities, which include a Gigabit Ethernet port and 2.5/5 GHz WiFi adapter, provide a way for owners to control, upload, and change the displayed content without the need to physically connect to the installation. In this chapter, you create a prototype of such a system. It will include a container orchestration service for easier updating and a simple online dashboard that will allow you to change the video and pictures displayed on the screen. See Figure 7-3.

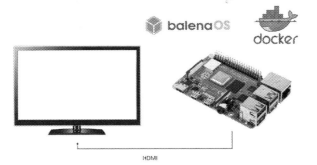

Figure 7-3. *Technology stack used in this chapter*

What Is (Docker) Container?

Docker is a technology for creating, deploying, and running applications by using containers. A *container* is an isolated, secure, lightweight environment that can be used to run any application. Containers are isolated from all the other containers on the host machine, as well as from the host operating system. Each container has its own filesystem, networking stack, and storage. The main benefit of using containers is the ability to run the same application on any machine, as well as to isolate each application from all other applications.

Containerization is one of the most important trends in the industry. With containers, you can create applications that run on any infrastructure. Containerization allows you to do all of this without having to worry about how the underlying infrastructure works. As long as your application can run in a container, it will work with any public or private cloud provider, or on your laptop.

Container Orchestration

Orchestration is where all the magic happens. Orchestration is the process by which software tools are used in order to automate tasks and make sure that your containers are behaving like you want them to behave. It is the practice of using multiple containers to achieve a higher goal. Orchestration is not just about running containers, it is about managing your entire container lifecycle. See Figure 7-4.

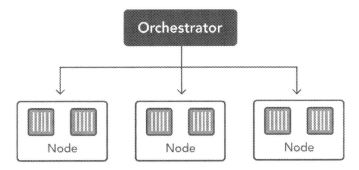

Figure 7-4. *The relationship between the orchestrator and the cluster nodes*

It includes creating the containers, starting them, stopping them, upgrading them, deleting them, linking them together to form an application, and scaling them up or down as traffic demands. Orchestrators are becoming increasingly popular because they make it easy to use containers in production environments. They provide an abstraction layer that makes it easier to deploy and manage clusters of containers without having to worry about the underlying infrastructure.

Balena.io for Container Orchestration

Balena.io is a container orchestration service that allows you to easily deploy and manage containers in a cluster, in a cloud, or in a datacenter. It supports both Docker and Rkt containers and provides a wide range of networking, storage, and security features, as well as monitoring and logging facilities. See Figure 7-5.

Figure 7-5. *Balena.io logo*

The platform is highly customizable and can be adapted to any use case. In this chapter you'll use Balena.io to deploy a Raspberry Pi 4 advertisement screen prototype based on BalenaOS, a minimal OS for running containers on embedded devices.

In order to display media files on the device, you'll use Balena Dash, which is a package that allows you to render any web page using a lightweight web browser. See Figure 7-6.

Figure 7-6. *Balena Dash logo*

This means that you can build a device dedicated to showing anything that runs in a normal web browser. It will boot up and automatically start displaying your content.

The container system that you'll be building consists of two main parts:

- A cluster of Raspberry Pi 4 devices running the BalenaOS operating system.

- An online dashboard from Balena that can be used to change the media content played on Raspberry Pis.

As mentioned, one of the more important aspects in setting up such a system is the ability to easily switch media to be displayed on the screen. In order to simplify adding new media files, we'll use an online dashboard tool that can be accessed from any web browser. The dashboard allows you to add media files and to send the upload request to the host controller service.

Implementation

You're going to perform the following steps to build this project:

1) Install BalenaOS on the Raspberry Pi 4 and connect the device to your account.

2) Deploy a container with Balena Dash to your device.

3) Set up the dashboard to display photos/videos.

Install BalenaOS

To install BalenaOS on your Raspberry Pi 4, go to `https://www.balena.io/` and create a free user account. The next step is to create a fleet.

A *fleet*, in cloud management terminology, is a group of devices that share the same architecture and run the same code. When you provision a device, it is added to a specific fleet, but can be migrated to another fleet at any time.

To create your first fleet, log in to your BalenaCloud dashboard and click the Create Fleet button, as shown in Figure 7-7.

Figure 7-7. *Fleet creation interface*

Select the Raspberry Pi 4 device type, choose a fleet type, enter a name, and click Create New Fleet. The name of the new fleet can be anything, but for the purposes of this project, it's called `digital-signage`.

Note   To create a fleet with multiple containers, you'll want to use the Starter or Microservices fleet type. The Starter fleets are full-featured and free for all users, with a limit of up to 10 total devices across all Starter fleets.

After the fleet has been created, you will be redirected to the dashboard for the newly created fleet, where you can add your first Raspberry Pi 4. See Figure 7-8.

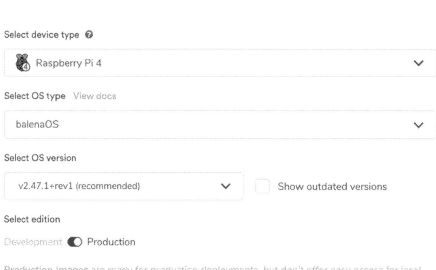

Figure 7-8.   Adding a new device to a fleet

For most fleets, you will have the option to select a device type. By default, the device type you chose when you first created the fleet will be selected. Fleets can, however, support any devices that share the same architecture, so you can choose another device type if needed.

After selecting a device type, select BalenaOS for the OS type; you will see a list of available BalenaOS versions. In general, you should use the most recent version available. You can also select whether to use a Development or Production edition with the respective toggle. Choose a Development image, as it has troubleshooting features enabled.

A toggle is also used to select whether your network connection will be through Ethernet only or with the WiFi + Ethernet option. Selecting WiFi + Ethernet allows you to enter a WiFi SSID and passphrase.

Once you have finished your image configuration, click the Download BalenaOS button. When the download completes, you should have a zipped file with a name like `balena-digital-signage-2.47.1+rev1-v10.6.27.img.zip`, where `digital-signage` is replaced with the name you gave your fleet on the dashboard.

The next step is to flash the downloaded image onto your SD card using Etcher, a simple, cross-platform SD card-writer and validator. Once you have Etcher installed, start it. To give Etcher access to your SD card, your system may prompt you to grant administrative privileges. See Figure 7-9.

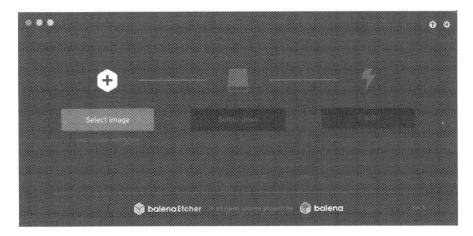

Figure 7-9. *Balena Etcher is used to flash an image to an SD card*

To create a bootable BalenaOS SD card, follow these steps:

1) Click Select Image and find your fleet's BalenaOS image file.

2) If you haven't already done so, insert your SD card into your computer. Etcher will automatically detect it. If you have more than one SD card inserted, you will need to select the appropriate one.

3) Click the Flash! button.

After the image finishes flashing, insert the SD card into your Raspberry Pi 4 and connect the Ethernet cable if necessary. Now power up the Raspberry Pi 4 by inserting the USB type-C cable. It will take a minute or two for the Raspberry Pi 4 to appear on your Balena dashboard. While you wait, the BalenaOS is expanding the partitions on your SD card to use all available space, installing a custom Linux environment, and establishing a secure connection with the Balena servers.

You should now be ready to deploy some code!

Deploy Container with Balena Dash to Your Device

Before you begin deploying the graphical interface to your Raspberry Pi 4, make sure that you have the necessary hardware. In practice, any screen will suffice. The easiest and most suitable option for advertisement display is connecting a large screen TV to a micro-HDMI port of the Raspberry Pi 4. Alternatively, you can use one of the 7-inch and 10-inch displays available, for example the official Raspberry Pi 7-inch touchscreen or the SunFounder 10.1-inch HDMI 1280x800 IPS LCD touchscreen for RPi 4. Once you have the display connected, you can start deploying the Balena Dash application to your cloud-connected device. See Figure 7-10.

Figure 7-10. *Balena logo displayed on a screen connected to a Raspberry Pi 4 with the Balena.io image*

Balena Dash is a Raspberry Pi powered digital photo/web frame that can display a fully GPU accelerated web page or app of your choosing; it allows you to update that content from anywhere. In order to deploy Balena Dash to your device, you need to install balena-CLI on the PC first.

Next are instructions for installing balena-CLI for most Linux distributions on Intel x86, such as Ubuntu, Debian, Fedora, Arch Linux, and other glibc-based distributions.

Download the latest ZIP file from the latest release page. It can be found in the balena-CLI GitHub repository (https://github.com/balena-io/balena-cli). Look for a file name that ends with -standalone.zip. For example:

balena-cli-vX.Y.Z-linux-x64-standalone.zip

Extract the ZIP file contents to any folder you choose, for example /home/james. The extracted contents will include a balena-cli folder.

165

Add that folder (e.g., /home/james/balena-cli) to the PATH
environment variable.

```
echo export PATH=\"\$PATH:/home/james/balena-cli\" >> ~/.bashrc
source ~/.bashrc
```

Check that the installation was successful by running the following
commands on a terminal window:

```
balena version - should print the CLI's version
balena help - should print a list of available commands
```

To update the balena-CLI to a new version, download a new release
ZIP file and replace the previous installation folder. To uninstall, simply
delete the folder and edit the PATH environment variable as described
previously.

When balena-CLI is installed, clone the Balena Dash repository to the
Chapter 7/ folder on your local PC with the following command:

```
git clone https://github.com/balenalabs/balena-dash
cd balena-dash
```

Log in to your Balena account with the following (see Figure 7-11):

```
balena login
```

Figure 7-11. *Successful login to the BalenaCloud account from Balena-CLI*

Then push the project to your device. Execute the following command from the `balena-dash` folder (see Figure 7-12):

```
balena push digital_signage
```

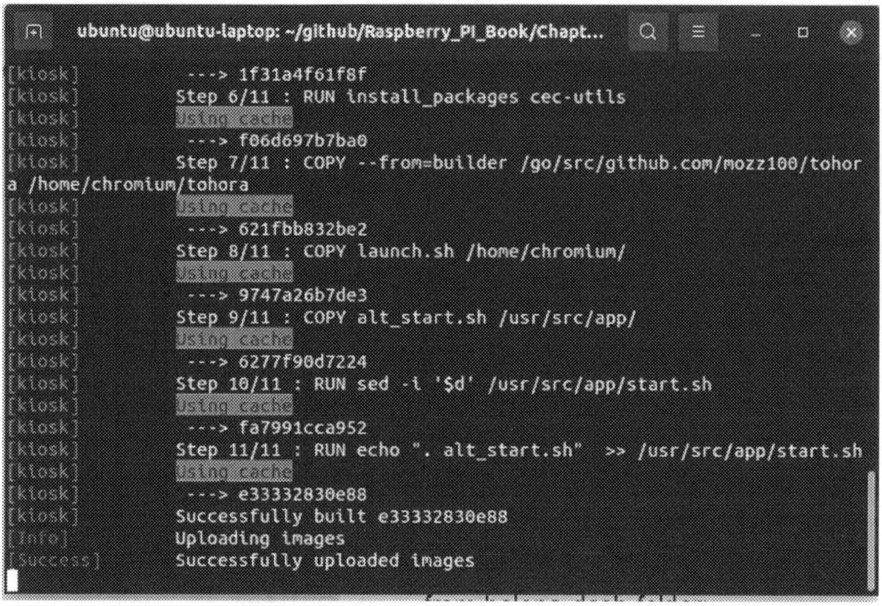

Figure 7-12. *Results of the balena push digital_signage command*

That command will push the source code of the project to BalenaCloud, build a container image there, and transfer it to the device.

While the image is being built and pushed to the device, add (or edit the existing) the device configuration variable BALENA_HOST_CONFIG_gpu_ mem. For this project, we recommend setting it to 128. You can add the device configuration variable by going to your Fleet page and choosing the Configuration tab. See Figure 7-13.

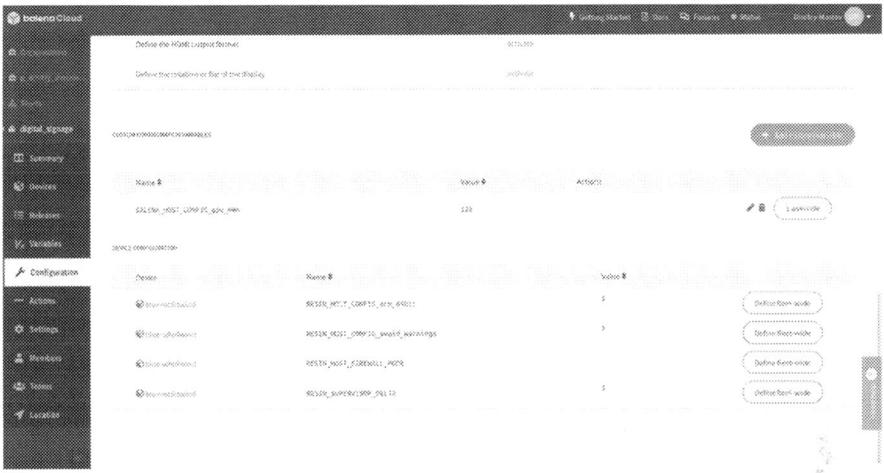

Figure 7-13. *BalenaCloud Fleet configuration page*

Once the installation procedure is finished, you will see the browser interface shown in Figure 7-14 on the screen connected to your Raspberry Pi 4.

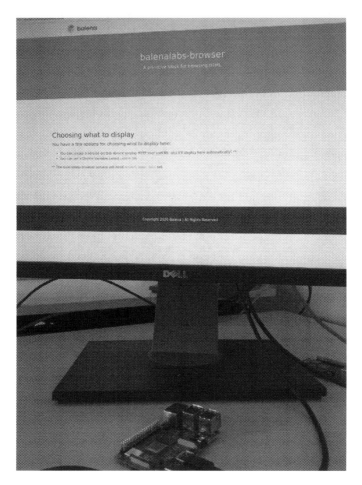

Figure 7-14. *Balena Dash start-up interface*

If you're seeing this output on your display, that means that everything is working and ready to go.

Right now the display is a blank canvas ready to show your content.

Set Up the Dashboard to Display Photos/Videos

You can choose any URL to be displayed on the screen. The easiest way to change the URL is to add a variable into the device variables inside BalenaCloud.

Click the device name on the Fleet page in BalenaCloud and then navigate to Device Variables. Click Add Variable and set the NAME as LAUNCH_URL and the VALUE as the URL you'd like Balena Dash to display. See Figure 7-15.

Figure 7-15. *BalenaCloud interface to changethe URL displayed on the advertisement screen*

Besides using YouTube, as in the initial example, you can easily set a video to automatically open in full screen and run on repeat.

To do this, you can use the service provided by yout-ube.com. This is as simple as finding the video you'd like to play and adding a - character after the t in the URL. For example let's choose an Adidas | Ready for Sport video (www.youtube.com/watch?v=Rwk5PdpTxSU). For that, you need to add www.yout-ube.com/watch?v=Rwk5PdpTxSU to the LAUNCH_URL parameter.

To change to a different video, alter the video ID in the URL. After about 30 seconds, the system will change the video that's played. See Figure 7-16.

Figure 7-16. *Balena Dash displaying a static image*

You can also serve static images or any other web pages by providing an image/web page URL to the LAUNCH_URL parameter.

Pro Tips

There are a few things that can be improved in the working solution you have now. First of all, you can develop an application-specific control dashboard that users can use to log in to and change the settings of the devices, without needing to know how the underlying container service works. That dashboard can be developed with Flask, a Python package you read about earlier for the vending machine control interface.

Another improvement possibly can be adding sensors to the system, which would allow it to react to environment changes. The simplest sensor addition would be PIR motion sensors, which allow the system to be triggered by the presence of people around it. See Figure 7-17.

Figure 7-17. *Seeed Studio's Grove Mini PIR motion sensor*

For more sophisticated scenarios, it is possible to analyze the number, age, and gender of people with the help of a camera and machine learning algorithms, similar to what's described in Chapter 2. Then the device can make adjustments to the content played on the screen, depending on predefined values and input from the machine learning algorithm.

Finally, on the hardware side, it is possible to create a minimalistic carrier board for the Raspberry Pi 4 Compute module, which would have a display port(s) and a USB for external device connection. The customized design would have both a smaller hardware footprint and be cheaper if produced in large quantities.

And of course, when actually deploying these screens to production in large quantities, security is paramount. IoT devices of all sorts, including digital signage screens, are increasingly becoming a target of cybercriminals.

Hardening your system's security might include:

- Protecting your data and services with encryption.

- Implementing a security policy about accessing data.

- Monitoring the system for unauthorized access and responding to potential threats.

- Using a VPN to encrypt and protect data in transit.

- Setting the device to only accept updates from a whitelist of IP addresses.

- Using network segmentation and isolation to limit the attack surface.

- Using the latest operating system with the most up-to-date security patches.

Summary

This chapter covered digital signage and showed you how to build a Raspberry Pi 4-based digital signage system using BalenaOS and Balena Dash. The digital signage is a device that displays a set of images and a video, with a loop that can be customized. Digital signage is a great way to generate new leads, increase business revenue, and increase brand awareness. You used BalenaOS to preinstall the Raspberry Pi. After that, the Balena dashboard was deployed to the Raspberry Pi 4 with the help of an online dashboard. The Balena dashboard allows you to upload media files on the Raspberry Pi 4 or display media files from the Internet.

CHAPTER 8

Cluster for a Web Application Hosting

Problem Overview

Modern businesses need to store and process large amounts of data: customer orders, inventory items, internal and external email correspondence, business website traffic, and so on. There are multiple ways to handle the IT operations associated with these activities and loosely they can be divided into the following:

- Using SaaS offerings from third parties

- Renting IT infrastructure from a public cloud company

- Creating and maintaining on-premises IT infrastructure by using resources within the company

And of course there is a way to mix and match these options, for example using SaaS (Software as a Service, a web app developed and serviced by a third party) for e-mail correspondence, hosting a database with Google Cloud SQL, and hosting a website on the company's internal web server. Creating and maintaining a company's own internal IT infrastructure has traditionally been available only to large companies,

© Elaine Wu, Dmitry Maslov 2022
E. Wu and D. Maslov, *Raspberry Pi Retail Applications*,
https://doi.org/10.1007/978-1-4842-7951-9_8

because of the high costs associated with renting a facility and purchasing the equipment and the expertise required to set up and manage an on-premise cloud. See Figure 8-1.

Figure 8-1. *Maintaining a company's own IT infrastructure used to require a large IT staff*

That has started to change in recent years with the advent of more powerful single-board computers and the help of software technologies, such as containerization, container orchestration, and clustering. They decrease the time needed to manage IT infrastructure and it is now possible for smaller businesses to run their own private cloud for a fraction of the cost of public SaaS solutions.

Business Impact

How does hosting an IT infrastructure on-premise benefit the company? There are multiple ways to answer this question. Here are a few of them.

- Data security: A company's local IT infrastructure can be designed in a way to provide superior data security in comparison to SaaS solutions. Unlike a public or hybrid cloud, a private cloud offers businesses full control over every aspect of the cloud infrastructure, as it is run on dedicated hardware rather than on a shared server. See Figure 8-2.

Figure 8-2. *Data security is of paramount importance to companies of all sizes*

All security efforts are deployed in-house or are outsourced to a managed service provider. Businesses don't need to share resources and can be certain their sensitive information isn't at risk of being exposed. This ownership, also known as single-tenant architecture, assures companies that their data is inaccessible to any unauthorized person.

- Better uptime: Due to the fact that SaaS solutions are hosted by third parties, their uptime is not in your control. SaaS solutions are usually more vulnerable to downtime than on-premises solutions. That is because third-party companies that offer SaaS solutions own the servers and not the company that uses the SaaS solution. The maintenance of the hosted infrastructure is therefore in the third-party's hands and they can choose when to do maintenance work, so in most cases the downtime is not announced in advance. Those third-party companies are also usually more susceptible to DDoS attacks (Volume Based Attacks, Protocol Attacks, Application Layer Attacks) than the company itself is, so in case of a DDoS attack, the company may experience downtime. Also, in most cases the downtime is not announced in advance. All that is not the case if you host your own infrastructure, so you can choose when to do maintenance work or upgrade your system and you can experience zero downtime in case of a DDoS attack.

- Lower costs: Public cloud solutions are usually more expensive in comparison to on-premises solutions. Comparing cloud vs. on-premise costs for small and medium-sized enterprises, an on-premises system can be more cost effective. Depending on the service you provide, the need to hold massive amounts of secure data or storage isn't always a requirement. On-premises can be an ideal solution for those who only want an initial investment for the system setup and maintenance costs can be kept to a minimum if scaling your business isn't your goal.

- Flexibility: If you choose to go with a public cloud solution, you will be limited by the way it is designed and offered by the provider. You will not be able to modify the hosted infrastructure in any way and that can be a problem if your business needs change. With on-premises infrastructure, that is not the case. You can scale up and down the infrastructure as needed and modify it in any way to fit your requirements.

- Control: With on-premises infrastructure, you have complete control over the infrastructure and your data. That makes it a safer and more reliable solution for the business. On-premises is where you can build purpose-built, customizable hardware systems that cater exactly to your company's needs. If consumer or market demands change, you have the option of customizing your offerings on site and can control the solutions.

While creating business IT infrastructure is a large topic that can well take a whole series of books to describe, this chapter creates a sample project—a hosting for a company website, with the help of a cluster of Raspberry Pi 4s. This solution allows for a high-availability system that's resilient to hardware failures and can be scaled according to demand.

Related Knowledge

Why would you build a Raspberry Pi cluster? This section goes a little deeper to understand the hype around Kubernetes, the uses of cluster computing, and the capabilities of MicroK8s. See Figure 8-3.

Figure 8-3. *Kubernetes and MicroK8s logos*

Kubernetes is a portable, extensible, open source platform for managing container workloads and services, and it facilitates both configuration and automation. If you run Kubernetes, you are running a Kubernetes cluster. A cluster contains a minimum of a worker node and a master node. The master is responsible for maintaining the desired state of the cluster, and the worker node runs the applications. This principle is the core of Kubernetes. Being able to break jobs down and run them in containers across any group of machines—physical, virtual, or in the cloud—means the work and the containers aren't tied to specific machines, they are "abstracted" across the cluster. See Figure 8-4.

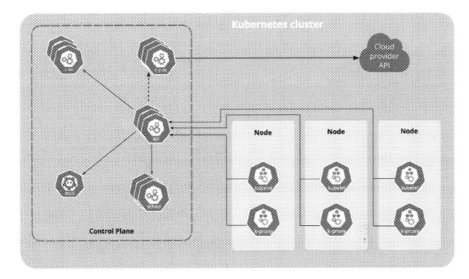

Figure 8-4. *Structure of a Kubernetes cluster*

Main Benefits of Running a Cluster with Kubernetes

The main benefits of running a cluster with Kubernetes for a business application, for example hosting a website or database locally, are the following:

- You can run your services on a cluster, instead of a single machine. A single machine might not have the processing power, memory, or storage to run your application. This is a big drawback for development purposes, as a large number of these services might be running on a single machine. With a cluster, you can run thousands of services on a much larger number of machines.

- Increase the flexibility and resilience of your application. For example, if one service fails,

181

Kubernetes can restart it. it. This is very important for a production business application, because if something goes wrong, you can restart it without any impact on your end users.

- Scale your application. If there is increased demand for your application, Kubernetes can scale up the number of services running on the cluster.

- Manage the life cycle of your services. Kubernetes allows you to start, stop, or restart your services. This is achieved by adding your services to a "pods" group. A pod is a group of one or more co-located containers, configured in a similar way, which can be deployed together on the same node. The pod ensures that the containers are deployed and managed together. When you want to update your service, you can do so by updating the pod. If there is a problem with one of the containers in the pod, Kubernetes can restart it.

- Minimization of the human effort required to maintain and scale the cluster. Kubernetes uses declarative configuration and API calls to manage the cluster. You write declarative configuration files for each of your services and Kubernetes does the work to keep the cluster running according to this configuration. Kubernetes provides a highly scalable, highly performant platform for developing and deploying containerized applications (and not only for Docker, but also for rkt, Singularity, and other container formats). It allows you to easily deploy and manage containerized application components and services, and to treat the complete application as a single, logical unit.

Deploying Kubernetes on the Edge with MicroK8s

If Kubernetes (K8s) is as good as everyone says it is, then the next thing to try is to apply the same model elsewhere. Somewhere where resources are heavily constrained and the management of computational resources is a performance-limiting factor. How about, at the edge?

MicroK8s is the most minimal, fastest version of K8s out there, and it includes the important features of a standard K8s cluster. It is optimized for the edge with hundreds of thousands of lines of codes taken out to be exactly what you need for managing devices. It makes single-(master)-node cluster deployments of Kubernetes easy to deploy for any purpose. There's no need to deploy a fully-blown production-grade cluster when you're prototyping or developing; you can test everything on MicroK8s before scaling. Here are some of the problems it solves:

- First, it gives you a Kubernetes cluster to play within seconds, so you can learn how it works. You can play with Kubernetes at your own pace without having to set up a big cluster.

- Second, it is super-small, so it boots up in seconds, which means you can start to use it when you need it. It's also much smaller than a full K8s cluster, so it can easily run on your device or your laptop.

- Third, it takes the guesswork out of installing Kubernetes. It's a single binary, so there's nothing to install, nothing to configure—just use it.

- Fourth, it's designed from the ground up for the edge, so it works well with resource-constrained devices. It enables you to run a Kubernetes cluster on a single machine, so you can get a full pods experience.

- Fifth, if you have a complex deployment, you can easily break it into small components that can be deployed independently, then glue them together for a complex deployment.

- Sixth, it lets you get your hands dirty with a real cluster, so you know what you're learning about works.

Implementation

In this chapter you're going to achieve the following:

1) Install Ubuntu Server 20.04 on two Raspberry Pi 4s.

2) Install MicroK8s on two Raspberry Pi 4s running Ubuntu Server 20.04.

3) Deploy a web application to a cluster.

Install Ubuntu Server 20.04 on Two Raspberry Pi 4s

While Kubernetes and by extension MicroK8s can be deployed to a multitude of different hardware platforms, the easiest installation can be achieved by using the Ubuntu 20.04 64-bit image for Raspberry Pi, which is available from the official Ubuntu website. The process of installing Ubuntu differs just slightly from the process of installing Raspberry Pi OS, described in Chapter 2.

First, insert the microSD card into your computer.

You then need to install the right Raspberry Pi Imager for your operating system. You can do this with the following links:

Raspberry Pi Imager for Ubuntu

Raspberry Pi Imager for Windows

Raspberry Pi Imager for macOS

Or, if you are on Ubuntu, you can run this comment:

```
sudo snap install rpi-imager
```

Once this is done, start the Imager and open the CHOOSE OS menu, shown in Figure 8-5.

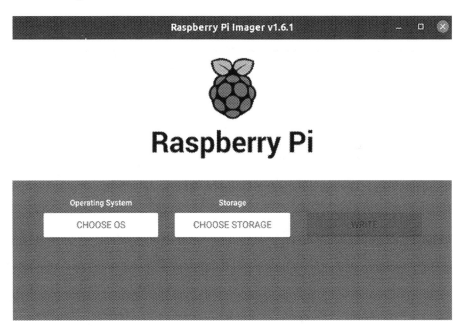

Figure 8-5. *Raspberry Pi Imager main menu*

Scroll down the menu and click Other General-Purpose OS, as shown in Figure 8-6.

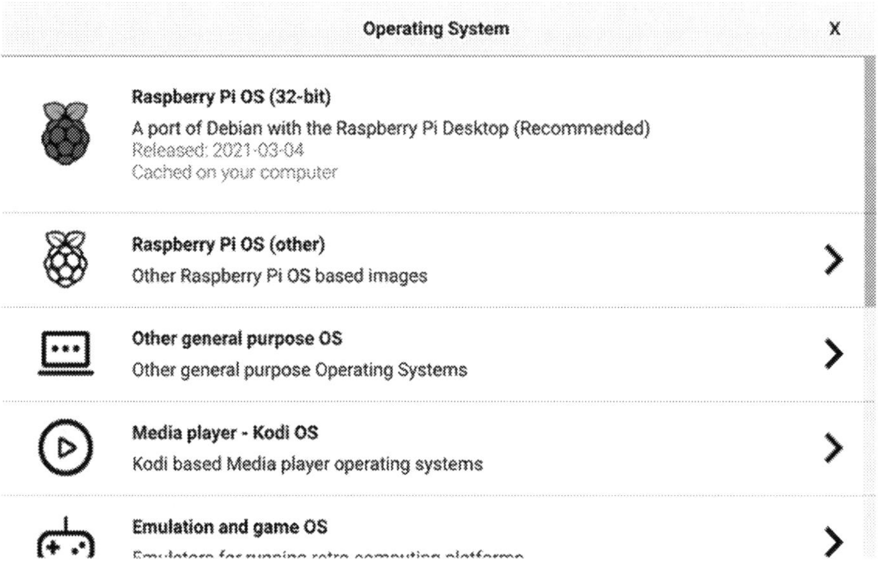

Figure 8-6. *OS selection menu*

Here you can select Ubuntu and see a list of download options. For this chapter, we recommend you select the Ubuntu 20.04 download. As indicated in the imager tool, this will work for the Raspberry Pi 3, 3+, and any of the 4s. See Figure 8-7.

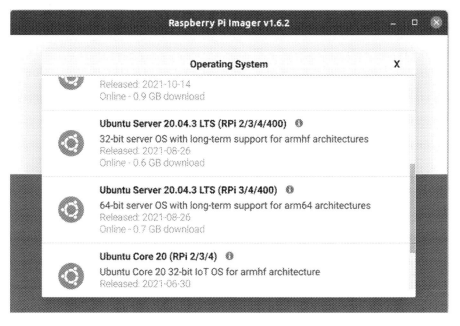

Figure 8-7. *Available options for Ubuntu*

Select the image and open the SD Card menu. Select the microSD card you inserted. See Figure 8-8.

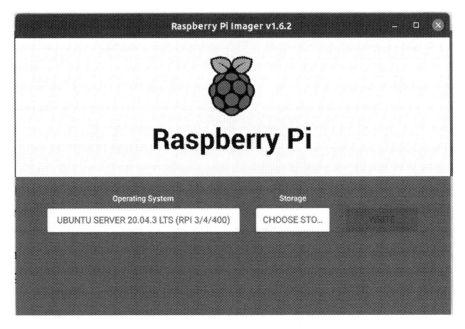

Figure 8-8. *Ready to choose storage and write*

Finally, click WRITE and wait for the process to finish.

For Ubuntu 20.04, you do not need to create an SSH file in the boot partition of the SD card. However, if you are using WiFi to access your Raspberry Pi, you still need to create a `network-config` file to add your WiFi credentials. The process is described in more detail in Chapter 2.

Warning   During your first boot, a tool called `cloud-init` does the configuration. Wait for it to finish before trying to log in. It typically takes less than two minutes, but there is a break between the login prompt and `cloud-init` completing. If you interrupt the process, you'll have to start again. You'll know it's done when it outputs some more lines after the login prompt appears.

Once cloud-init finishes, log in using SSH with ubuntu as both the password and the login ID. The first login should be done using the command line, since the OS will ask you to change the default password. After the default password has been changed, you can SSH into the machine using your favorite IDE. The procedure for using Visual Studio Code is described in Chapter 2.

Install MicroK8s on Two Raspberry Pi 4s Running Ubuntu Server 20.04

Follow this section for each of your Pis. Once it's completed, you will have MicroK8s installed and running everywhere.

SSH into your first Pi. There is one thing you need to do before you start with MicroK8s deployment. You need to enable c-groups so the kubelet will work out-of-the-box. To do this, you need to modify the configuration file /boot/firmware/cmdline.txt:

```
sudo nano /boot/firmware/cmdline.txt
```

And add the following options:

```
cgroup_enable=memory cgroup_memory=1
```

The full line for this particular Raspberry Pi looks like this:

```
cgroup_enable=memory cgroup_memory=1 net.ifnames=0 dwc_otg.
lpm_enable=0 console=ttyAMA0,115200 console=tty1 root=/dev/
mmcblk0p2 rootfstype=ext4 elevator=deadline rootwait
```

Now save the file in your editor and reboot:

```
sudo reboot
```

Once that's done, you can Install the MicroK8s snap:

```
sudo snap install microk8s --classic
```

Figure 8-9 shows the successful installation.

```
ubuntu@ubuntu:~$ sudo snap install microk8s --classic
2020-02-21T10:45:19Z INFO Waiting for restart...
microk8s v1.17.2 from Canonical✓ installed
```

Figure 8-9. *Successful installation of MicroK8s*

What Version of Kubernetes Is Being Installed?

MicroK8s is a snap and as such it will be automatically updated to newer releases of the package, which closely follows upstream Kubernetes releases.

To follow a specific Kubernetes upstream series, it's possible to select a channel during installation. For example, to follow the v1.17 series:

```
sudo snap install microk8s --classic --channel=1.17/stable
```

Channels are made up of a track (or series) and an expected level of stability, based on the MicroK8s releases (Stable, Candidate, Beta, Edge).

Discovering MicroK8s

Before going further, let's take a quick look at the MicroK8s command line. The start command will start all enabled Kubernetes services:

```
microk8s.start
```

The inspect command will give you the status of services:

```
microk8s.inspect
```

The stop command will stop all Kubernetes services:

```
microk8s.stop
```

You can easily enable Kubernetes add-ons. For example, to enable kubedns, run this command:

```
microk8s.enable dns
```

To get the status of the cluster, run this command:

```
microk8s.kubectl cluster-info
```

Before joining the second Raspberry Pi to the cluster, you need to change the hostnames from default ubuntu to something unique. You can achieve that by typing the following and changing the hostname in the file:

```
sudo nano /etc/hostname
```

For this chapter, we use ubuntu-master for the master node and ubuntu-worker1 for the first leaf node.

Note   To conform with notation used in most tutorials on the Internet (which are written for the MicroK8s full-fledged version, or just simply Kubernetes), we assign an alias to the MicroK8s application.

To do that, append these two lines to the end of the .bashrc file on both of your Raspberry Pi 4s:

```
export PATH="$HOME/.local/bin:$PATH"
alias kubectl='microk8s kubectl'
```

Then run the following:

```
source ~/.bashrc
```

Deploy a Web Application to a Cluster

In the context of Kubernetes, a "node" is a machine that is running the Kubernetes control plane and is managed by the master. A node is also referred to as a "worker node".

A "pod" is a group of one or more containers that run on a "node" and share resources such as storage and network.

A "service" is a set of "pods" that perform a related function. Services are more abstract than pods and are intended to be more long-lived. Services provide a single IP address and port that can be load-balanced. "Deployments" are used to describe the desired state of Kubernetes. They dictate how pods are created, deployed, and replicated.

"Labels" are key/value pairs that are attached to resources (like pods) and are used to organize related resources. You can think of them as CSS selectors.

An "ingress" is a set of routing rules that control the external access to "services" based on the request host or path.

"Volumes" are used to persist data beyond the life of a container. They are especially important for stateful applications like Redis and Postgres. In Kubernetes, a "persistent volume" is a virtual block device or file with a predetermined size that can be attached to a pod. When a pod is created, a persistent volume claim is created to request the use of a persistent volume. The persistent volume claim and the persistent volume are bound together, and the persistent volume is mounted on the pod.

To create a new object in Kubernetes, you must provide a "spec" that describes its desired state.

For example:

```
apiVersion: apps/v1kind: Deploymentmetadata:
  name: flaskspec:
  replicas: 1
  template:
    metadata:
      labels:
        app: flask
    spec:
      containers:
```

```
- name: flask
  image: mjhea0/flask-kubernetes:latest
  ports:
  - containerPort: 5000
```

The variables are defined as follows:

- `apiVersion`: The version of the Kubernetes API that the object was created with.

- `kind`: A string value representing the REST resource this object represents. Servers should convert recognized values into appropriate concrete resource identifiers before performing a request.

- `metadata`: An ordered map of string-valued keys and JSON strings as values.

- `spec`: Fields that describe the desired state of the object.

In this example, this `spec` will create a new deployment for a Flask app with a single replica (pod). Take note of the containers section. Here, we specified the Docker image along with the container port the application will run on.

Persistent Volume and Persistent Volume Claim

Again, since containers are ephemeral, we need to configure a volume, via a `PersistentVolume` and a `PersistentVolumeClaim`, to store the Postgres data outside of the pod.

Note   The files and directories described here are located in the `Chapter_8` directory.

Take a look at the YAML file in kubernetes/persistent-volume.yml:

```
apiVersion: v1kind: PersistentVolumemetadata:
  name: postgres-pv
  labels:
    type: localspec:
  capacity:
    storage: 2Gi
  storageClassName: standard
  accessModes:
    - ReadWriteOnce
  hostPath:
    path: "/data/postgres-pv"
```

This configuration will create a hostPath PersistentVolume at /data/postgres-pv within the node. The size of the volume is 2GB, with an access mode of ReadWriteOnce, which means that the volume can be mounted as read-write by a single node.

Create the volume:

```
$ kubectl apply -f ./kubernetes/persistent-volume.yml
```

View the details:

```
$ kubectl get pv
```

You should see:

Figure 8-10. *Created persistent volume*

```
kubernetes/persistent-volume-claim.yml:
apiVersion: v1kind: PersistentVolumeClaimmetadata:
  name: postgres-pvc
  labels:
```

```
  type: localspec:
 accessModes:
   - ReadWriteOnce
 resources:
   requests:
     storage: 2Gi
 volumeName: postgres-pv
 storageClassName: standard
```

Create the volume claim:

```
$ kubectl apply -f ./kubernetes/persistent-volume-claim.yml
```

View details:

```
$ kubectl get pvc
```

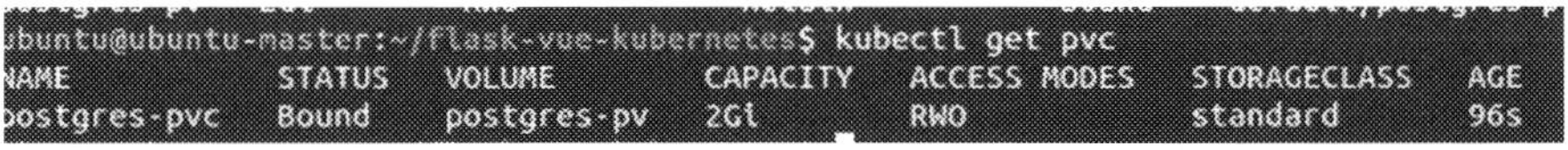

Figure 8-11. *Volume claim status*

Secrets

You can store sensitive information in a secret object. For example, you can store a database password in a secret object. A secret object is a special type of object that is used to store sensitive information. For this project, it is stored in a file called secret.yml. The secret object contains multiple fields:

```
apiVersion: v1
kind: Secretmetadata:
  name: postgres-credentials
type: Opaque
data:
  user: c2FtcGxl
  password: cGxlYXNlY2hhbmdlbWU=
```

The user and password fields are base-64 encoded strings (security via obscurity):

```
$ echo -n "pleasechangeme" | base64cGxlYXNlY2hhbmdlbWU=
```

```
$ echo -n "sample" | base64
c2FtcGxl
```

The secret object uses base-64 encoding and plaintext strings to store the sensitive information.

Add the Secrets object:

```
$ kubectl apply -f ./kubernetes/secret.yml
```

Postgres

With the volume and database credentials set up in the cluster, you can now configure the PostgreSQL database.

```
kubernetes/postgres-deployment.yml:
apiVersion: apps/v1kind: Deploymentmetadata:
  name: postgres
  labels:
    name: databasespec:
  replicas: 1
  selector:
    matchLabels:
      service: postgres
  template:
    metadata:
      labels:
        service: postgres
    spec:
      containers:
      - name: postgres
```

```
    image: postgres:13-alpine
    env:
      - name: POSTGRES_USER
        valueFrom:
          secretKeyRef:
            name: postgres-credentials
            key: user
      - name: POSTGRES_PASSWORD
        valueFrom:
          secretKeyRef:
            name: postgres-credentials
            key: password
    volumeMounts:
      - name: postgres-volume-mount
        mountPath: /var/lib/postgresql/data
  volumes:
  - name: postgres-volume-mount
    persistentVolumeClaim:
      claimName: postgres-pvc
  restartPolicy: Always
```

This is a Kubernetes configuration file for deploying a PostgreSQL database. The PostgreSQL image is pulled from DockerHub. The user and password for the database are stored in a secret (which is not shown here). The PostgreSQL data directory is mounted into the container. The pods are created by the Deployment controller.

This is a more advanced topic, but the controller watches the Kubernetes API for new pods and automatically schedules them onto nodes in the cluster. The pod is a group of containers that are scheduled together. The PostgreSQL container is what actually runs the database. The Deployment controller will create one pod for this deployment. The pod will have one replica, which means it will be scheduled onto one node in the cluster. The replica count is set to 1, so the `Deployment` controller will schedule one pod onto one node. All pods in a deployment must have the same number of replicas, and the `Deployment` controller will schedule those replicas onto nodes in the cluster.

The `matchLabels` line means that the pod will only be scheduled onto nodes that have these labels: `service: postgres` The `template` line means that the pod will be created from this template. The template contains the configuration for the PostgreSQL database. The `volumeMounts` line mounts a persistent volume into the PostgreSQL container. This persistent volume is created by a `PersistentVolumeClaim`. The `PersistentVolumeClaim` creates a claim that can be used by pods in this deployment. The `restartPolicy: Always` line tells the `Deployment` controller to always restart the pod if it fails. The PostgreSQL container is the one that runs the database. The PostgreSQL data directory is mounted into the container.

Finally, when applied, the volume claim will be mounted into the pod. The claim is mounted to `/var/lib/postgresql/data`—the default location—while the data is stored in the `PersistentVolume`, `/data/postgres-pv`.

Create the deployment:

```
$ kubectl create -f ./kubernetes/postgres-deployment.yml
```

Here's the status:

```
$ kubectl get deployments
```

Figure 8-12. *Deployments status*

```
kubernetes/postgres-service.yml:
```

```
apiVersion: v1
kind: Service
```

```
metadata:
  name: postgres
  labels:
service: postgres
spec:
  selector:
    service: postgres
  type: ClusterIP
  ports:
  - port: 5432
```

The service has a label called `service` and another label called `type`. The `type` label has the value called `ClusterIP`. `ClusterIP` is a special type of IP address, which is used by Kubernetes to route traffic to the correct pod. The `selector` label defines how to route traffic to the pod. The selector could be based on a resource type, such as an ingress (or `LoadBalancer`), or a pod label. In this case, it is based on the `service` label. The service type is a ClusterIP, so the selector will route traffic to the correct pod based on the service label.

The port `5432` is the port that the container exposes. The container runs a PostgreSQL database, so it has a port for PostgreSQL. If you have a PostgreSQL client, you can connect to this port and communicate with the database. You can also connect to the port from outside of Kubernetes, but you will need to know the IP address of the database. The IP address is the IP address of the pod that contains the database. The IP address is a ClusterIP, which is a special type of IP address used by Kubernetes to route traffic to the correct pod.

Since the service type is ClusterIP, it's not exposed externally, so it's only accessible from within the cluster by other objects.

Create the service:

```
$ kubectl create -f ./kubernetes/postgres-service.yml
```

Create the books database using the pod name:

```
$ kubectl get pods
```

```
ubuntu@ubuntu-master:~/flask-vue-kubernetes$ kubectl get pods
NAME                        READY    STATUS     RESTARTS    AGE
postgres-668b84984b-dczkx   1/1      Running    0           3m22s
```

Figure 8-13. *The pod with PostgreSQL database*

```
$ kubectl exec postgres-xxxxxxx-xxxxx --stdin --tty --
createdb -U sample books
```

Note   Of course, you need to change `postgres-xxxxxxx-xxxxx` to the name of pod you see after running the `get pods` command. This change applies to the following instructions as well.

Verify the creation:

```
$ kubectl exec postgres-95566f9-xs2cf --stdin --tty --
psql -U sample
```

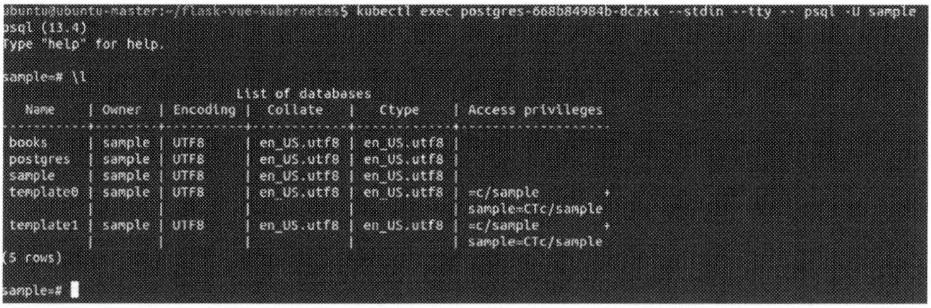

```
ubuntu@ubuntu-master:~/flask-vue-kubernetes$ kubectl exec postgres-668b84984b-dczkx --stdin --tty -- psql -U sample
psql (13.4)
Type "help" for help.

sample=# \l
                                   List of databases
   Name    | Owner  | Encoding |  Collate   |   Ctype    | Access privileges
-----------+--------+----------+------------+------------+-------------------
 books     | sample | UTF8     | en_US.utf8 | en_US.utf8 |
 postgres  | sample | UTF8     | en_US.utf8 | en_US.utf8 |
 sample    | sample | UTF8     | en_US.utf8 | en_US.utf8 |
 template0 | sample | UTF8     | en_US.utf8 | en_US.utf8 | =c/sample        +
           |        |          |            |            | sample=CTc/sample
 template1 | sample | UTF8     | en_US.utf8 | en_US.utf8 | =c/sample        +
           |        |          |            |            | sample=CTc/sample
(5 rows)

sample=#
```

Figure 8-14. *Database in the container*

Type exit and press Enter to exit the interactive PostgreSQL prompt.

You can also get the pod name using the following:

```
$ kubectl get pod -l service=postgres -o jsonpath="{.items[0].
metadata.name}"
```

Assign the value to a variable and then create the database:

```
$ POD_NAME=$(kubectl get pod -l service=postgres -o
jsonpath="{.items[0].metadata.name}")
$ kubectl exec $POD_NAME --stdin --tty -- createdb -U
sample books
```

Flask

Next, you're going to create the Flask deployment:

```
$ kubectl create -f ./kubernetes/flask-deployment.yml
```

And create the service for it:

```
kubectl create -f ./kubernetes/flask-service.yml
```

Why do you need to create a service for every deployment? The service provides a way to access a deployment. Deployments cannot be accessed without a service. You can think of the service as an entry point to your application. When you create a deployment, you create a pod. If you want to access your application, you need to bind the service to an external IP address. So if you want to access your application from outside of your cluster, you need to create a service for it. The service will be bound to an external IP address and the pods will be accessible through that IP address. You can also access your pods through their internal IP addresses, but that's only useful if you want to access them from within your cluster. The service is also used to check if the pods are healthy.

Apply the migrations and seed the database:

```
$ kubectl get pods
```

```
ubuntu@ubuntu-master:~/flask-vue-kubernetes$ kubectl get pods
NAME                         READY   STATUS    RESTARTS   AGE
postgres-668b84984b-dczkx    1/1     Running   0          27m
flask-7496f9747-49nsd        1/1     Running   0          4m20s
```

Figure 8-15. *Flask pod status*

```
$ microk8s.enable dns
$ kubectl exec flask-xxxxxx-xxxxxx --stdin --tty -- python
manage.py recreate_db
$ kubectl exec flask-xxxxxx-xxxxxx --stdin --tty -- python
manage.py seed_db
```

Verify:

```
$ kubectl exec postgres-xxxxxx-xxxxxx --stdin --tty --
psql -U sample
```

```
ubuntu@ubuntu-master:~/flask-vue-kubernetes$ kubectl get pods
NAME                         READY   STATUS    RESTARTS   AGE
postgres-668b84984b-dczkx    1/1     Running   0          30m
flask-7496f9747-49nsd        1/1     Running   0          6m57s
ubuntu@ubuntu-master:~/flask-vue-kubernetes$ kubectl exec postgres-668b84984b-dczkx --stdin --tty -- psql -U sample
psql (13.4)
Type "help" for help.

sample=# \c books
You are now connected to database "books" as user "sample".
books=# select * from books;
 id |               title                |    author     | read
----+------------------------------------+---------------+------
  1 | On the Road                        | Jack Kerouac  | t
  2 | Harry Potter and the Philosopher's Stone | J. K. Rowling | f
  3 | Green Eggs and Ham                 | Dr. Seuss     | t
(3 rows)

books=#
```

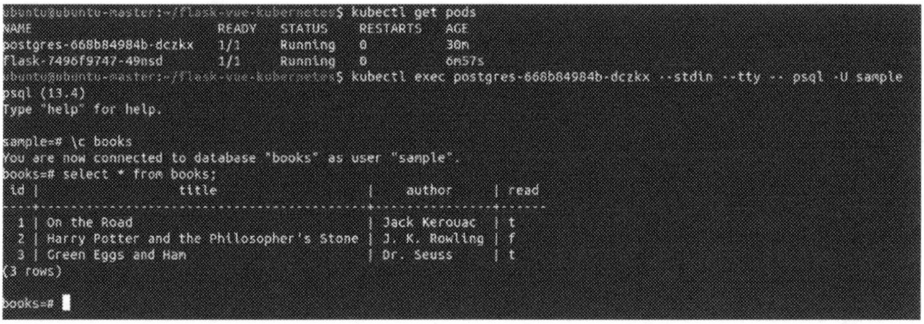

Figure 8-16. *Sample from the database*

Ingress

The Ingress controller is a sidecar container that proxies and translates HTTP requests to the application containers. It's like a reverse proxy. It is the only way to expose an application to the outside world. The Ingress controller watches the Kubernetes API for new services and automatically configures itself to route traffic to those services.

In `minikube-ingress.yml`, we defined the following HTTP rules:

> / routes requests to the Vue service (which you need to set up)

> /books routes requests to the Flask service

Enable the `ingress` add-on:

```
$ microk8s.enable ingress
```

Create the `ingress` object:

```
$ kubectl apply -f ./kubernetes/minikube-ingress.yml
```

Next, you need to update your `/etc/hosts` file to route requests from the host you defined, `hello.world`, to the MicroK8s instance. First check your Raspberry Pi 4 IP address with the `ifconfig` command:

```
$ ifconfig
```

It normally will be something similar to 192.168.1.108.

Add an entry to your computer's (not Raspberry Pi 4) /etc/hosts:

```
$ echo "$(your-rpi-IP hello.world" | sudo tee -a /etc/hosts
```

Then try it out by accessing the following addressees with your computer's browser:

`http://hello.world/books/ping` (see Figure 8-10).

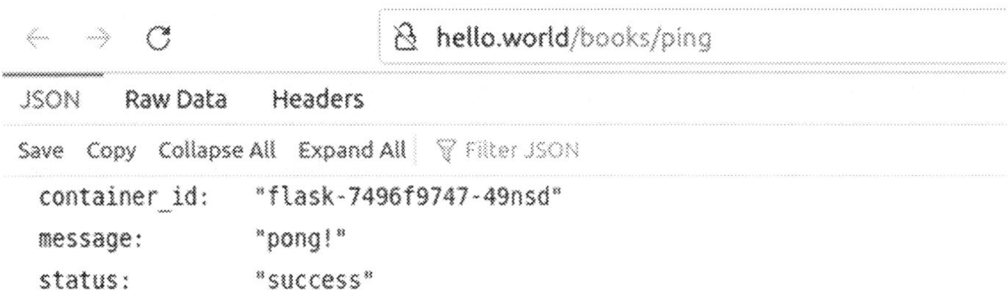

Figure 8-17. *Result of accessing the address in a PC's web browser*

`http://hello.world/books` (see Figure 8-11).

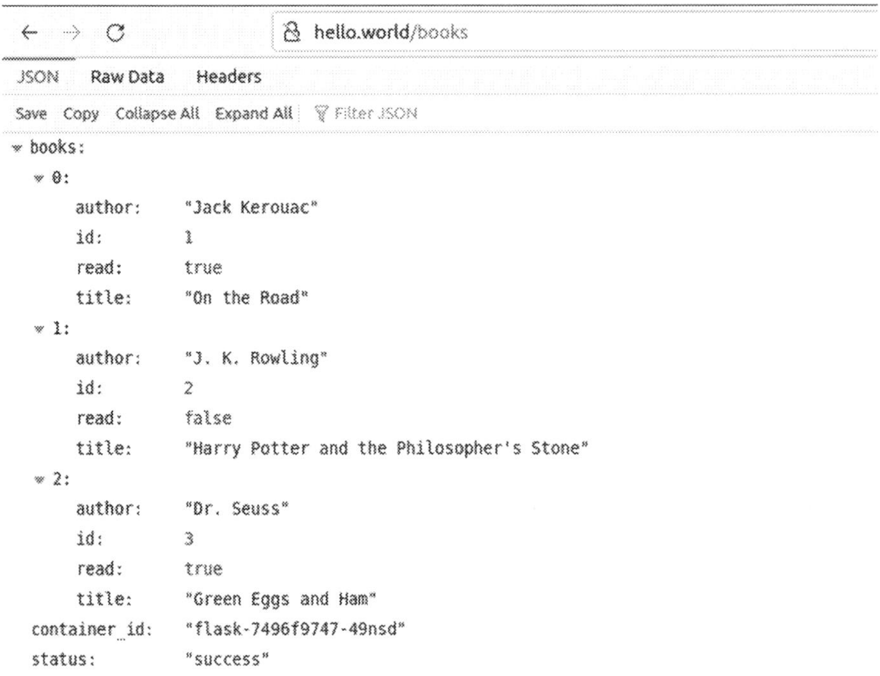

Figure 8-18. *Result of accessing the address in a PC's web browser*

Vue

Vue is a front-end framework that is used to create single-page web applications. It is similar to React in terms of usage, but uses a different template syntax. It is easy to learn and the syntax is simple. Vue is used in combination with other frameworks like React, Angular, or even with jQuery. It can be used to create single-page applications, but can also be used to create pages with multiple pages, like a blog. Vue is easy to learn and use. It has a simple syntax that allows you to create dynamic web pages quickly. It has a strong focus on the view layer only.

Create the deployment:

```
$ kubectl create -f ./kubernetes/vue-deployment.yml
```

Verify that a pod was created along with the deployment:

```
$ kubectl get pods
```

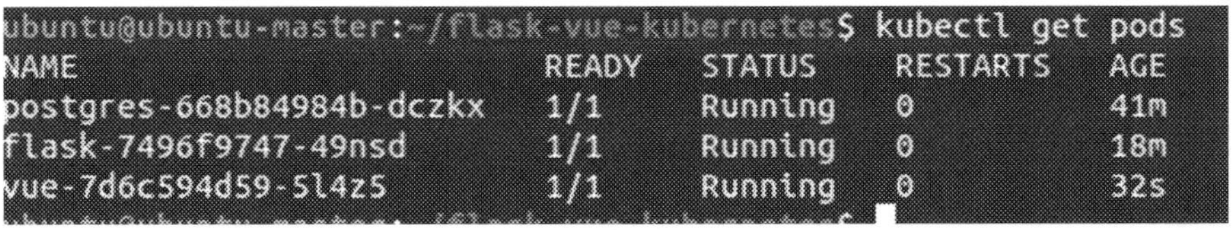
ubuntu@ubuntu-master:~/flask-vue-kubernetes$ kubectl get pods
NAME READY STATUS RESTARTS AGE
postgres-668b84984b-dczkx 1/1 Running 0 41m
flask-7496f9747-49nsd 1/1 Running 0 18m
vue-7d6c594d59-5l4z5 1/1 Running 0 32s

***Figure 8-19.** Newly created Vue pod status*

Create the service:

```
$ kubectl create -f ./kubernetes/vue-service.yml
```

Ensure `http://hello.world/` works as expected by going to that page in your computer's browser. See Figure 8-12.

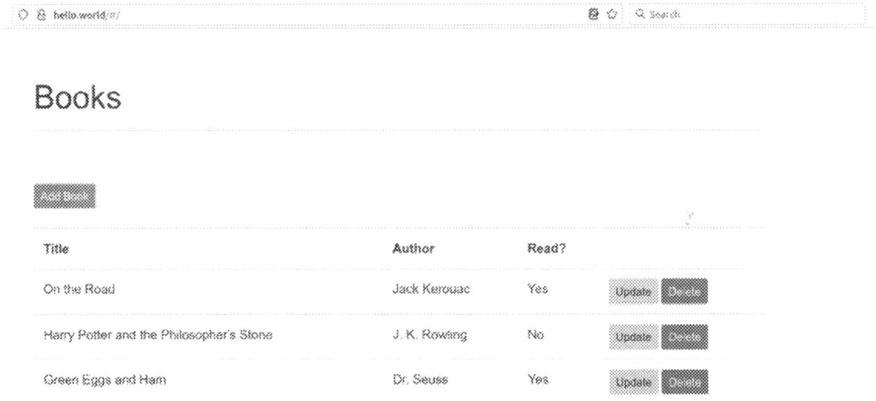
Books
Title
Author
Read?
On the Road
Jack Kerouac
Yes
Harry Potter and the Philosopher's Stone
J. K. Rowling
No
Green Eggs and Ham
Dr. Seuss
Yes

***Figure 8-20.** Working web application on a MicroK8s cluster consisting of a single Raspberry Pi 4*

Scale and Add Nodes

Kubernetes makes it easy to scale, adding additional pods as necessary, when the traffic load becomes too much for a single pod to handle. The pods will be distributed across nodes in the cluster to better handle the load.

On your first (master) Raspberry Pi, execute the following:

```
$  sudo microk8s.add-node
```

This command will generate a connection string in the form of
`<master_ip>:<port>/<token>`.

Figure 8-21. *Connection string generated by master node*

Now you need to run the `join` command from the Pi that you want to
add to the cluster:

```
microk8s.join <master_ip>:<port>/<token>
```

For example:

Figure 8-22. *Joining new node to the cluster*

For each new node, you need to run the `microk8s.add-node` command
on the master, copy the output, then run `microk8s.join <master node
output>` on the leaf.

When you have two nodes, you can add another three Flask pods to the
cluster as follows:

```
$ kubectl scale deployment flask --replicas=4
```

Confirm:

```
$ kubectl get deployments flask
```

Figure 8-23. *Scaling up the flask nodes*

```
$ kubectl get pods -o wide
```

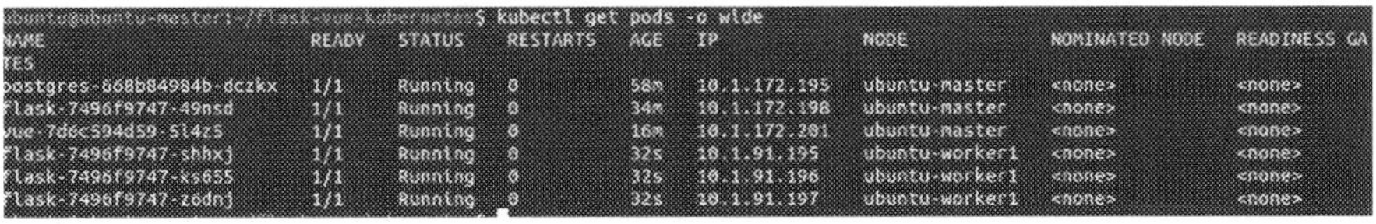

Figure 8-24. *Additional flask nodes status*

Make a few requests to the service from your computer:

```
$ for ((i=1;i<=30;i++)); do curl http://hello.world/books/
ping; done
```

You should see different container_ids being returned, indicating that requests are being routed appropriately via a round-robin algorithm between the four replicas:

Figure 8-25. *Replies recieved from different pod replicas*

Pro Tips

After completing the project in this chapter, you have a scalable web application running on a cluster of two Raspberry Pis. Following these same principles, you can extend the application to host a website or even an online store. If you add two more devices to this cluster, it becomes a HA (highly available) cluster. A highly available Kubernetes cluster is a cluster that can withstand a failure on any one of its components and continue serving workloads without interruption. There are three components necessary for a highly available Kubernetes cluster:

- There must be more than one node available at any time.

- The control plane must be running on more than one node so that losing a single node would not render the cluster inoperable.

- The cluster state must be in a datastore that is itself highly available.

Additional nodes in the cluster also will help in maintaining swift response time when you have a large amount of clients accessing the web application at the same time.

While the web application created in this chapter can only be accessed from the local network, it is fairly trivial to set a domain name purchased on one of the websites, such as godaddy.com or namycheap.com, to point at the IP address of the cluster, so it becomes available to clients on the Internet.

Finally, when deploying your cluster to production, it is important to pay attention to security, both within the cluster and when it interacts with the Internet. There are a number of ways to enhance security when using a Kubernetes cluster. One is to require all communications between Kubernetes nodes be secured using TLS/SSL. This can be done by configuring Kubernetes to use TLS/SSL for all communications, or by configuring Kubernetes to use TLS/SSL for communications between nodes and the API server.

Another way to enhance security is to use role-based access control (RBAC). This can be done by creating roles and assigning specific permissions to those roles. Then, you can assign users or groups to those roles. This will give those users or groups the permissions specified in the role. You can also use pod security policies to enhance security. Pod security policies allow you to specify which containers can run on a particular pod and what privileges they have. This can help to prevent unauthorized access to sensitive data or to the Kubernetes API. Finally, you can use network security controls to help secure the network traffic between nodes and pods. Network security controls can help prevent unauthorized access to data and to the Kubernetes API.

Summary

MicroK8s is a single-node Kubernetes cluster that enables you to get a complete Pods experience. It's a small, self-contained binary that runs on a single machine. It is designed from the ground up for the edge, so it works well with resource-constrained devices. It takes the guesswork out of installing Kubernetes by being a single binary that you can run. It enables you to run a Kubernetes cluster on a single machine, so you can get a full pods experience. It lets you get your hands dirty with a real cluster, so you know that what you're learning about actually works. It also makes it easy to break up complex deployments into smaller components, so you can test individual components before deploying them together. You learned how to set up the MicroK8s cluster on two Raspberry Pi 4s and how to run a simple web application with a database that can be further extended to be accessible from the Internet.

CHAPTER 9

Summary and Tips on Practical Implementation

In previous chapters, you have learned how the Raspberry Pi brings digital transformation to retail businesses and how to build prototypes to optimize human and machine resource allocation and streamline your business operations. The book's prototype projects included a vending machine, a smart touchscreen-enabled directory, a speech recognition drive-thorough, an employee-management system, an advertisement display, a people-counting camera, and a cluster server for hosting the company's IT infrastructure.

Raspberry Pi has gained widely acclaim, especially among makers and Linux enthusiasts, for the same reasons that it makes an ideal hacker-friendly gadget: its hardware is flexible and can be adapted to handle Internet surfing, retro gaming, learning about computers, and setting up home servers. The Raspberry Pi first launched ten years ago and it now has new customers, including manufacturers and business owners who have found it to be an affordable, practical, low-maintenance device for running their companies' infrastructures. See Figure 9-1.

© Elaine Wu, Dmitry Maslov 2022
E. Wu and D. Maslov, *Raspberry Pi Retail Applications*,
https://doi.org/10.1007/978-1-4842-7951-9_9

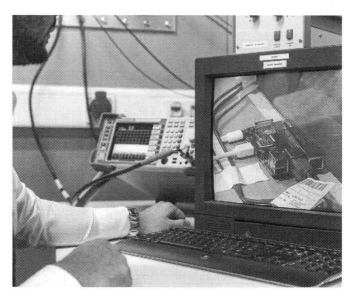

Figure 9-1.   *Raspberry Pi is gaining adoption in industry, after of years of being a hobbyist-oriented device*

Successful Implementations

In this last chapter, we expand a bit on the projects' implementations and give you additional technical and business advice that will help you when creating your own Raspberry Pi-powered application.

Raspberry Pi Vending Machine

According to tomshardware.com, iSnowfall (Reddit ID), in the final year's project for students with special needs, has produced a 1.8-meter-high and .5-meter-wide vending machine powered by Raspberry Pi. It uses RFID cards for transactions. The RFID UID number is stored on a database on a Google sheet via a Python script. Once the Raspberry Pi confirms the points received, it drives the motor to deliver the selected products. See Figure 9-2.

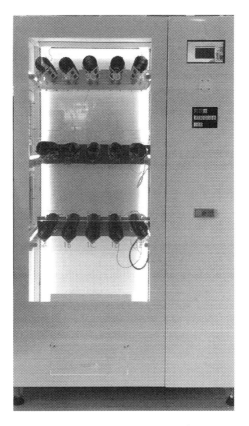

Figure 9-2. *Raspberry Pi vending machine (Credit: iSnowfall)*

The vending machine uses a PCB integrated with Raspberry Pi Compute Module and other essential component boards and accessories. You can also attach a Hat with all the functions you need on the Raspberry Pi.

Upstate Networks Inc. (UNI), a hardware and software manufacturer from New York, used the Raspberry Pi to develop vending machine peripherals. Since 1994, UNI has designed adapters that bridge vending machines and standardized computers. On the UNI website, you will find a product line called PLUM, which is an unattended sales system integrated with a Raspberry Pi-embedded controller. See Figure 9-3.

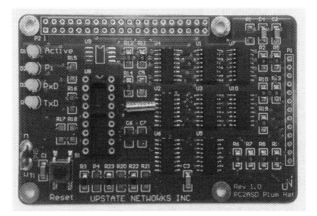

Figure 9-3.   *Upstate Networks Inc.'s PLUM payment system works with the Raspberry Pi single-board computer*

PLUM comes with three extension boards for use with the Raspberry Pi: PLUM-IN, PLUM-OUT, and PLUMPicker:

- PLUM-IN enables a vending machine protocol called multi-drop bus (MDB) when it is used with Raspberry Pi. MDB is used by various devices such as dollar bill validators, coin acceptors, and coin dispensers. The system allows the Raspberry Pi to process the incoming funds.

- PLUM-OUT allows the Raspberry Pi to be used as a cashless device when combined with any MDB vending product.

- PLUMPicker is a Raspberry Pi HAT for item selection process on the shelf. When PLUM-IN is attached to the Raspberry Pi, the touchscreen can be used instead of the hardware keyboard to handle the project selection process. If you plug PLUMPicker into the reTerminal, you can directly use the HMI device to interact with the vending machine. Once the Raspberry Pi is connected to the Internet, PLUMPicker can also bridge the vending machine and the message from the cloud for remote control or the command sent from the HMI device.

Interactive Touchscreen Directory for a Smart City

There are more than 8,000 locals and tourists visiting Coogee Beach in Australia. There are awesome bars, restaurants, promenades, and parks everywhere. In 2018, the Randwick City Council adopted a smart city strategy seeking to improve livability, sustainability, and economic prosperity through digitalization and IoT. This strategy established a roadmap to guide and accelerate the smart city action in Randwick. The Randwick Smart Beach Project faces the challenge of creating a better beach experience: applying public safety, traffic, parking management, facility maintenance, and all open data on the beach with a public dashboard. In this case, Coogee Beach adopted Ubidots to create dashboards to view sensor results and control devices in real time. See Figure 9-4.

Figure 9-4. *Smart display with live data from Coogee Beach, source: Ubidots*

To develop a custom dashboard, you can simply populate the dashboard with prebuilt graphs, charts, plug-ins, indicators, maps, and control units, or use HTML Canvas and custom code.

Figure 9-5 shows that Peclet developed a digital display and integrated all these tools in Ubidots. The display shows the data from all IoT sensors placed around Coogee Beach. The sensor data is transmitted through LoRa used with the LoRaWAN web server through "The Things Network".

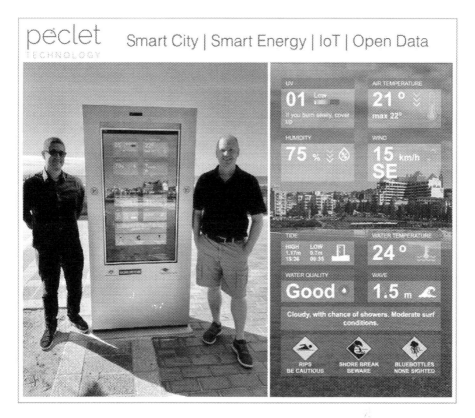

Figure 9-5. *Example of data displayed on the device, source: Ubidots*

Raspberry Pi as a Retail Product Display

Digitec is an electronics retailer in Switzerland. Among other things, they sell Raspberry Pis and related accessories, including their official 7-inch touch display. Many customers might have noticed that they haven't had the touch display in stock recently, and there's an interesting reason for that. See Figure 9-6.

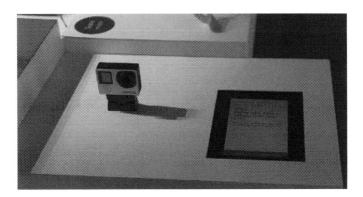

Figure 9-6. *Touchscreen display used in Digitec stores in Switzerland, source: Raspberry Pi*

The retailer wanted to replace their tablet-based digital shelf labels with something more robust, so they turned to Raspberry Pi 2 with the 7-inch touchscreen. Each store has 105 screens, which means that the engineering team for Digitec Galaxus assembled 840 custom-printed Raspberry Pi-powered shelf labels to replace the existing paper-based product labels. See Figure 9-7.

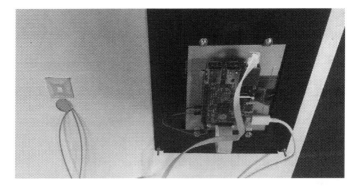

Figure 9-7. *The back side of the touchscreen display installation, source: Raspberry Pi*

The screens enable their customers to view up-to-date product information, prices, and customer opinions based on community ratings as they see the product up close. To pull this off, the engineering team used Raspbian Jessie Lite and installed the Chromium browser. It enabled them to create a custom HTML page that loads JavaScript to download the most up-to-date information using a JavaScript Ajax call. When a keyboard is connected, it can set parameters for the screen, which are stored as cookies in Chromium. The engineering team also introduced unnecessary redundancies into the design. For example, the boot script will put Chromium in a loop to ensure that it will eventually be relaunched if it crashes. It is also capable of handling sudden loss of power and network connectivity issues.

A Multimedia Toolkit for Museums, Visitor Centers, and More Running on the Raspberry Pi

Pi Presents is a toolkit for producing interactive multimedia applications for museums, visitor centers, and more.

There are a number of digital signage solutions for the Raspberry Pi, which are generally browser based, limited to slideshows, non-interactive, and driven from a central server, thus enabling the content to be modified frequently. See Figure 9-8.

Figure 9-8. *Examples of Raspberry Pi used in museum installations, source: Raspberry Pi*

Pi Presents is different. It is standalone, multimedia, highly interactive, and diverse in its set of control paradigms—slideshows, cursor controlled menus, radio buttons, and hyperlinked shows. It's able to interface with users or machines over several types of interfaces. It is aimed primarily at curated applications in museums, science centers, and visitor centers.

219

Being so flexible, Pi Presents needs to be configured for your application. This is achieved using a simple-to-use graphical editor; it needs no Python programming. There are numerous tutorial examples and a comprehensive manual.

Pendulum Wave Machine: A Museum Exhibit

The University of Florida Physics Department has a lobby exhibition which is very reminiscent of the Discovery Gallery in the London Science Museum. One of their latest exhibits is a Pendulum Wave Machine. They used the GPIO and animation facilities of Pi Presents to provide tightly coupled user interaction with the machine. See Figure 9-9.

Figure 9-9. *A museum exhibit made with Raspberry Pi*

John from the Physics Department describes how it works:

> "It runs Pi Presents Gapless version 1.3 on a Raspberry Pi 2 board. The application has a main slideshow that runs non-stop until a guest presses the Start button. Starting triggers a sub-show slideshow that also controls the state of the machine so it stays in sync with the show. We use three GPIO pins for switches, one to start the machine by viewers and

trigger the sub-show off of the main show, and two micro switches that tell us the position of the machine (its state). We also use one GPIO pin for driving the electrical motor that operates the machine."

Raspberry Pi 4 Cluster for Hosting a Raspberry Pi 4 Website

An 18-board Raspberry Pi 4 cluster was used to host much of the official raspberrypi.org website on its busiest day. The recently released 4GB Pi 4 costs $55, a fraction of the cost of traditional server hardware, but is also less powerful and offers less memory than entry-level servers. Mythic Beasts, the ISP that hosts the Raspberry Pi website, configured the cluster to serve most of the website and found it handled record demand on the day of Pi 4's release without issue. See Figure 9-10.

Figure 9-10. *Cluster of 18 Raspberry Pi 4s used to serve the raspberrypi.org website on the day of the Raspberry Pi 4 launch, source: Arstechnica*

The cluster consisted of the following elements:

- 14× dynamic web server (PHP/Apache)

- 2× static web server (Apache, flat files)

- 2× memcache (in memory store to accelerate web serving)

221

The Raspberry Pi foundation ran the website on this Raspberry Pi 4 cluster for over a month before reverting back to the usual virtual server-based environment.

Technical Know-Hows

This section discusses technical know-hows related to the various projects covered in this book.

Use Virtual Network Computing (VNC) to Remotely Control Everything You Want to Execute on the Raspberry Pi

Sometimes it is not convenient to work directly on the Raspberry Pi or access it using SSH with Visual Studio Code or OpenSSH client. If you want to edit the code from another device and need to access the graphical user interface of Raspberry Pi, we suggest trying RealVNC for accessing a remote desktop. VNC is a graphical desktop remote-sharing system that allows you to remotely control the desktop interface of a computer (running the VNC server on the Raspberry PI) from another computer or mobile device (running the VNC viewer on your laptop). See Figure 9-11.

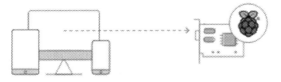

Figure 9-11. *RealVNC: connect to your Raspberry Pi from anywhere*

You will be able to see and control the Raspberry Pi desktop in a window on your computer.

VNC Connect from RealVNC is already included in the Raspberry Pi OS Desktop version. Download the VNC Viewer from their website first to the device you want to use to remotely control your Raspberry Pi, such as your Mac, Windows machine, or Linux P. See Figure 9-12. Then you can use the following simple tutorial to enable VNC and use it on your Pi.

Figure 9-12. *Download VNC View from their website*

Make your PC join the same private local network as your Raspberry Pi (for example, an Ethernet or WiFi network).

On your Raspberry Pi, discover the private IP address by double-clicking the VNC Server icon or running `ifconfig` from the terminal. See Figure 9-13.

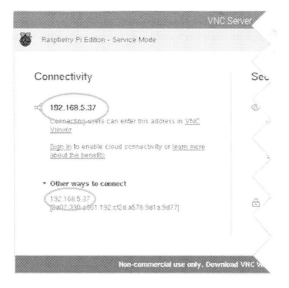

Figure 9-13. *Raspberry Pi IP address displayed in the VNC server window*

On your PC, run VNC Viewer and enter the IP address that you just found for the Raspberry Pi in the search bar, as Figure 9-14 shows. After successful connection, you will see the Raspberry Pi desktop on your PC. You are now ready to use your development board remotely with access to the graphical user interface!

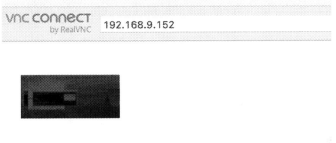

Figure 9-14. *Type the IP address into the VNC Viewer*

IoT Integration Platform for the People-Counting Project

Chapter 2 introduced computer vision and deep learning, which were used to develop a people-counting application. However, in order to include an end-user friendly dashboard that can deliver all the data you want to analyze for the decision makers' benefit, you need to merge the physical camera results with the digital analysis into one user interface.

Thousands of IoT entrepreneurs, startups, and system integrators are using Ubidots to rapidly launch and scale Internet of Things (IoT) businesses without having to write code. An IoT integration platform will save you a lot of time and money when creating and testing a visualized operation dashboard that connects multiple hardware devices. The complexity of deploying an end-to-end complete IoT solution goes far beyond the application prototype, which requires a variety of IoT technologies such as hardware compatibility, communication, software, and UI interfaces. If you have confirmed that the best solution is using hardware, a connection, and the cloud—such as using a Raspberry Pi connected to the cloud via WiFi—you still need to develop an application to provide data to your customers and control all the devices from the visualized dashboard.

For IoT applications, the last layer involves backend and frontend components, and it usually takes thousands of engineering hours to deliver a stable solution with a flexible UI interface. In order to quickly assemble and launch IoT applications, you can choose an IoT integration platform like Ubidots, which has both hardware and software options and efficient integration tools. See Figure 9-15.

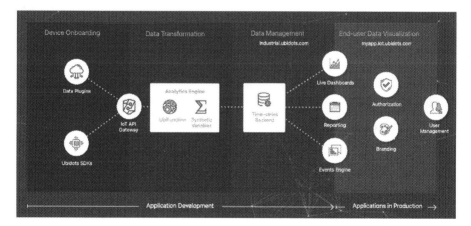

Figure 9-15. *IoT application development workflow, source: Ubidots*

Real-world data is critical to digital transformation. How to collect and process data remains a challenge for system integrators, device providers, business-end users, and many stakeholders. For retailers, it is still difficult to use automation and digitalization to drive their businesses from ideas into practice. End-to-end IoT solution platforms, such as Seeed, help retailers and end users accelerate and scale their IoT solutions from hardware end to user end, offering real-world data collection from nodes, edge devices connection with multiple communication choices, data operation at the cloud, and SaaS and PaaS to achieve digital transformations. See Figure 9-16.

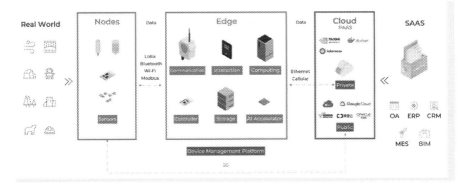

Figure 9-16. *Top-level overview of the IoT infrastructure stack, source: Seeed*

Choosing an IoT integration or solution platform can speed up retail business automation transformation. Its low cost and power consumption usually are essential to business retailer facilities as vending machines and customer service directional devices.

Microphone Options for Speech Recognition

Different microphone options in Raspberry Pi have many factors to take into account, including size, cost of development, and maintenance cost. This makes voice recognition design more challenging. While any microphones can work for your proof of concept (PoC), they will likely produce poor-quality results with your Raspberry Pi voice recognition software.

To overcome these challenges, Seeed Studio provides the reSpeaker USB microphone array, as shown in Figure 9-17. It offers a better voice pick up, which is essential when you place the drive-through machine outside the restaurant. The reSpeaker USB microphone array supports up to 5m far-field voice pickup and 360° pickup mode, and it implements the following acoustic algorithms: DOA (Direction of Arrival), AEC (Automatic Echo Cancellation), AGC (Automatic Gain Control), and NS (Noise Suppression).

Figure 9-17.   *Seeed Studio's reSpeaker USB microphone*

Cluster Server Carrier Board

As mentioned in Chapter 8, Raspberry Pi 4 is capable of serving a website to millions of visitors, if several boards are combined together in a cluster. While it is feasible to build a cluster yourself, just like we did for the prototype project, by connecting Raspberry Pi 4s with Ethernet cables, Turing Pi offers a better alternative, called a "cluster on board." There are two models of Turing Pi currently on the market: Turing Pi 1 supports Compute Modules 1, 3, and 3+, and the upcoming Turing Pi 2 also supports Compute Modules 4. See Figure 9-18.

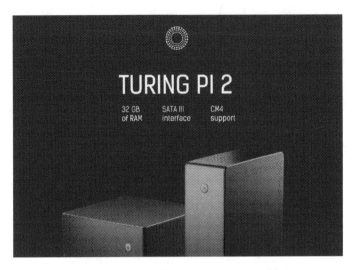

Figure 9-18. *Turing Pi 2 concept drawing*

Turing Pi is a compact ARM cluster kit that provides a secure and scalable compute in the edge. It is designed to make edge computing easier for developers. Turing Pi cluster architecture allows you to migrate and sync web apps with minimal friction.

Turing Pi includes dedicated I/O connections for the first slot, so you can manage the entire cluster through a Pi in one slot, or you can use another computer to manage the entire cluster externally. You only need to plug in the power supply, keyboard, and mouse (or the power supply and network cable) and you are ready to use it! See Figure 9-19.

Figure 9-19. *Turing Pi 1 Cluster carrier board*

Retail Business Digitalization

Retailers have been experiencing major shifts in the last decade. The online shopping and e-commerce market is growing and expanding and physical stores and shopping malls are becoming less and less attractive to many customers. The digitalization of retail business can be achieved by integrating various technologies and innovative business solutions. The idea of digitalization is to make the business as efficient as possible and provide personalized customer experiences driven by customer demand. The journey to digitalization requires a lot of time and effort, as there are many issues to be solved. Digitization represents a continuous transformation that is very important to the retail industry. Digital transformation empowers retailers in multiple ways, with hardware technology combined with the latest software technology such as pretrained AI models, digital twins, and AR, VR, 360 video, 3D, and so on. Consider these tips:

- **Know your customers precisely:** Identify, adjust, and meet customer changing demands. There are shopping malls now that have deployed cameras with built-in AI models to accurately read customer expressions and analyze satisfaction.

- **Use more efficient and smarter tools to provide excellent customer service and collect reliable data:** For example, you can use the Raspberry Pi to deploy all the advertising posters as well as collect all feedback reports of all the advertisements and shops in a large shopping mall. See Figure 9-20.

Figure 9-20. *Microsoft Cloud for Retail, source: Microsoft*

- **Deliver the supply chain intelligently, with digital and physical real-time interactions:** In the retail industry, digital twins may help supply chains and stores with real-time intelligent communication. Real-time sensors are deployed in warehouses and retail stores to obtain device data and connect ERP databases through the network. Digital twins can help retailers identify supply shortages in seconds. You can use IoT to obtain data from the physical world and connect it to the cloud. Based on the digital twins technology, you can define and create a custom model that simulates the real environment in any field based on the data. In these models, the highly integrated platforms can predict and make corresponding executions to optimize the workflow, analyze assets, track inventory locations, and ensure employee's safety. See Figures 9-21 and 9-22.

Figure 9-21. *Building a digital twin for a retail store, source: SAP*

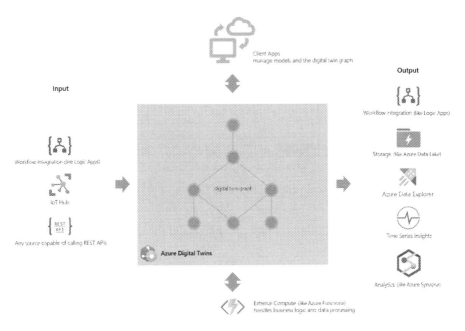

Figure 9-22. *Microsoft Azure digital twins*

We introduced Amazon Dash Cart in Chapter 1 and the application of a Raspberry Pi-powered dictionary in a shopping mall in Chapter 4. Can you use digital twin technology to combine these two ideas? Gathering the image captured by the cameras in the shopping basket and on the goods shelf, as well as data from the motion sensor, you could create an interactive model of the shopping basket on the shelf. These models can analyze the best placement of goods on the shelves and the customers' preferences. At the same time, the screen on the basket can recommend promotional items from other shelves close to customers. See Figure 9-23.

Figure 9-23. *Veeve Intelligent Carts are powered by computer vision and deploy seamlessly into existing stores with no additional retrofit required. Source: Veeve*

Similar to Dash Cart, Veeve also provides a contactless checkout experience by integrating computer vision into existing shopping carts in grocery stores. Retail in-store service staff need to have the right information, training, and convenient tools to provide customers with a superior customer service experience. Grocery stores using Veeve also offer employees a tablet with access to all shopping carts for real-time customer support. See Figure 9-24.

Figure 9-24. *The Raspberry Pi development board family continues to grow*

Here are some tips on how to implement digitalization in your retail business:

1. **Before you start, make sure that your business is ready for digitalization.** There are many things to consider, including the size of your business, the marketing strategy, the customer base, the level of competition, and so on.

2. **Define your goals and plan your business transformation.** Make sure that you have clear goals and plan how you are going to reach them.

The failure to plan is planning to fail. Plan your business transformation, create milestones, set a budget for the project, define the metrics, and monitor the progress. The plan should be flexible enough to allow for changes, but rigid enough to serve as an important guide to keep you on track. Make sure that the plan has a clear direction and that it answers the main question of why you are going through all this effort in the first place.

3. **Select the technologies that you want to implement.** This is one of the most important steps in the process of digitalization. Many technologies are available, but not all of them are suitable for your business. Therefore, make sure that you select technologies that will be beneficial for you and your clients.

4. **Implement your plans.** The implementation phase is the most important part of the process. This is where you actually digitize your business. You can start by automating some of the tasks and processes in your business. Make sure that you do not make hasty decisions and implement only what is really necessary.

5. **Measure your progress.** You should track the progress of your digitalization project. See Figure 9-25.

Figure 9-25. *Setting metrics and evaluating the progress according to them is very important for staying on track with the original plans*

Make sure that you set goals and have developed metrics.

6. **Revise your strategy.** After some time, you should revisit your strategy and revise it. The digitalization of your business should be a continuous process. You should not stop after the first implementation. Try to improve the processes and technologies that you have already implemented and add new ones.

Additionally, think of future-proofing your business. The idea of digitalization is to keep your business progressive and competitive in the long-term. This requires a serious commitment and a lot of time and effort. However, it is a good idea to future-proof your business at the same time. Keep in mind that not all technologies will last forever. It is a good idea to apply technologies and solutions that will be reliable and of high quality and that will provide long-term benefits to your business. See Figure 9-26.

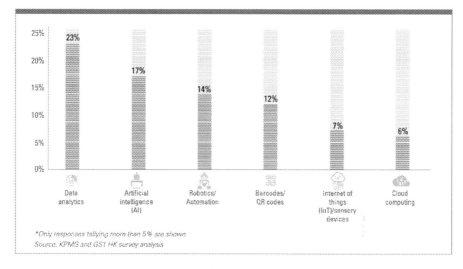

Figure 9-26. *Most important digital technology for businesses in the next two years. Source: KPMG, Digital Retail on the Rise*

Digitalizing a retail business requires a lot of time and effort. However, it is a journey worth taking, as the results are worth the effort. Digitalization will bring new customers to your business, will increase your sales, and will make your business more competitive.

With the popularity of the Raspberry Pi board, more businesses are catching on, including local eateries in Spain, city governments in Quebec and Oakland, CA, and FedEx in Thailand, Belgium, Japan, Tennessee, and Philadelphia. These examples show how Raspberry Pi computers can be entrenched in geographical landmarks, both physical and virtual. Retail businesses can save costs, which can be passed to customers, while providing high levels of structure, security, and flexibility. Small and medium retail businesses, for example, restaurants and cafes, can also benefit from using Raspberry Pi computers, as they can turn their business into a digital retail business.

Companies that have already deployed Raspberry Pi-based systems in airports, malls, parking lots, railway stations, offices, and hotels can leverage the feedback of their customers to further improve their products and services. See Figure 9-27.

Figure 9-27. *A digital signage screen made with Raspberry Pi and powered by Binary Emotions OS*

The functionality of the applications varies from business to business, but all of them share the same capacity to offer unprecedented levels of flexibility, convenience, and quality. Quality of service is critical for retail customers and retail business digitalization greatly improves it by elevating the level of service while reducing costs.

In conclusion, we hope that the detailed, step-by step projects described in this book and the examples of real-world implementations show you how powerful and versatile Raspberry Pi computers can be in transforming your retail business with digitalization. The Raspberry Pi-based system is safe, secure, and highly flexible, with limited risk of failure. Raspberry Pi-based systems can be incorporated into any retail business, regardless of the size of the business, the type of goods and services it offers, the number of customers, the geographic location, and even the type of physical environment it operates in.

Index

© Elaine Wu, Dmitry Maslov 2022
E. Wu and D. Maslov, *Raspberry Pi Retail Applications*,
https://doi.org/10.1007/978-1-4842-7951-9

F

Fingerprint sensor
  AS608 sensor
    built-in UART, 136
    GPIO pinout guide, 138
    header files, 137
    scanner module, 135
    USB-to-serial
      converter, 136
  attendance.csv file, 145
  database, 147
  searching option, 142
  enrollment process, 141
  error message, 141
  grove base hat, 143
  integrated optical modules,
    131, 132
  main menu, 140
  motion sensor objects, 144–149
  USB-to-serial converter, 140
Flask web server
  boilerplate code, 58
  elements, 60
  html template, 60
  learning process, 58
  main.html file, 60
  mobile phone browser, 63
  payment option, 64
  PayPal checkout, 64
  pyqrcode, 59
  python server.py, 59
  success.html template, 62
  success route function, 60

G

Graphical user interface (GUI), 77
  button widget, 84
  logical program, 86
    export interface, 86
    project structure, 87
    reTerminal, 89
    show_label() method,
      87, 88
    zara_button code, 87, 88
  mall map set, 84
  PAGE GUI generator, 81–83
  position and attributes, 85
  widget toolbar, 83–85
Grove Balena.io, mini PIR motion
  sensor, 173

H

Human machine interface (HMI),
  2, 73, 75

I, J

Industry 4.0
  deloitte definition, 4
  development process, 1
  industrial revolutions, 2
  IoT (*see* Internet of
    Things (IoT))
  manufacturing process, 2
  pandemic crises, 3
  single-board computers, 4

Printed in the United States
by Baker & Taylor Publisher Services